INDIA ANTHROPOLOGY

INDIA ANTHROPOLOGY

By

Dr. S. Narayan

GYAN PUBLISHING HOUSE
New Delhi - 110002

Indian Antropololy

ISBN : 978-81-212-0235-0

Published, 2016

Published in India by

Gyan Publishing House
5, Ansari Road
Daryaganj, New Delhi-110002
Phone: 9811692060
E-mail: books@gyanbooks.com
Webside: gyanbooks.com

Printed at: G. Print Process, Delhi.

PREFACE

Anthropology, the science of man, has been rightly said to be the mirror of man. The present work of mine i.e. Indian Anthropology, reflects the diverse problems of the Indian social system with special reference to Tribal India. The tribals are diverse in their nature, composition and problem. The plan, policies and approaches for their development need anthropological insight. We have to win their confidence. We should reconsider our role. Are we really helping them or are we getting 'help' in the pretension of extending them 'help'. Most of the plans and policies are not target oriented rather are 'executors oriented'. Thus, those who are professing the science of man in its totality in India need to search their heart honestly. This heart-searching may give a new perspective to Indian anthropology. However, we have developed to a stage at which we may call that we have 'Indianness' in the science of man. I do not wish to go into further intellectual jargons and controversies but simply wish to state that the subject needs real identification with man in India. It should play its diagnostic as well as prescriptive role. It is a sad affair that even at this stage the subject is not that popular as it shou d be

I am thankful to my mother Smt. Shakunthala Devi v no has always encouraged me for my lofty ideas. My special tnank goes to my wife Mrs. Shobha Narayan and to our children Shiwani, Subhas and Savidh for their constant help in their own way. I am also thankful to Sri K.G. Narayan, B.K. Narayan, Dhirendra Narayan, Satyendra Narayan, Shekhar, Brindaban Prasad. Sinha, Madan Mohan Prasad Sinha, Sachchidanand Prasad Sinha, Vijay Kumar Sinha, Binay Kumar Sinha and Alokanand Prasad, Anil Kumar Sinha, and Sushil Kumar

Sinha for their help which they extended me in completing this work.

I am specially thankful to the administration of the A.N. Sinha Institue without whose cooperation this would not have been possible. I am sincerely thankful to Mr. M.J. Philip, who took keen interest in typing the script of this book.

Hope this will serve the long awaited book in anthropology, specially for the students as it is based on the syllabi of U.P.S.C., M.A. and M.Sc. of the Indian Universities.

A.N. Sinha Institute of Social Studies
Patna

SACHINDRA NARAYAN

CONTENTS

1

GROWTH AND CONCEPTS

The Growth

Indian Anthropology owes its origin to the Asiatic Society of Bengal, which was established in 1774 by Sir William Jones to study "nature and man". Since last two hundred years, Indian Anthropology has marched ahead and attempts have been made by anthropologists in the past viz. Roy (1922), Dubey (1962) Bose (1963), Majumdar (1950, 1956) and Vidyarthi (1966, 1978) to classify the course of development in terms of the dominant trends in anthropological investigation. While it was too early for S.C. Roy (1922) to classify the ethnographic studies in terms of time perspective, he simply categorised them in terms of the sources of publications i.e. magazines, handbooks, monographs etc. He also attempted to identify the nationality of the authors who conducted investigation among different tribes and castes in India. Again, S.C. Dube (1962) and N.K. Bose (1963) also did not make any explicit attempt to categorise the anthropological materials in terms of meaningful historical sequences. However, the attempts of Majumdar (1956) and late Prof. L.P. Vidyarthi (1966, 1978) to make scientific classification of different phases of Indian Anthropology were quite significant. Borrowing terms of T.K. Penniman (1935), D.N. Majumdar, for the first time divided the anthropological researches in India into three phases viz.

The formulatory—1774—1911

Constructive—1912—1937 and

Critical—1938—onwards.

In the determination of the beginning of the formulatory period, however, the establishment of the Asiatic Society of Bengal, was the only choice as it marked the beginning of the the scientific study of "nature and man" in India. According to Majumdar, the beginning of the second phase is, obviously, marked with the publication of the first full length monograph on MUNDA AND THEIR COUNTRY (1912) by Sir S.C. Roy, "the father of the Indian Anthropology". The beginning of the period from 1938, known as the critical period, as put forward by Majumdar, coincides with the Silver Jubilee Celebration of the Indian Science Congress when many foreign anthropologists including B.K. Malinowaski had come to India and created an atmosphere of critical studies of Indian tribes and castes. Thus, Majumdar called it the beginning of an era which has shown a critical approach.

The most significant classification of the rise and development of Indian anthropology has been made by late Prof. L.P. Vidyarthi (in two volumes) in 1978. Although he had already published some preliminary observations on social anthropological researches in India (in the Journal of Social Research Vol. 9, No. 1) in 1966, but it took him several years to write a very comprehensive history of Indian Anthropology, covering almost all the branches of this discipline, which finally came out in 1978.

While Vidyarthi (Ibid) agreed with his teacher, D.N. Majumdar about the beginning of the formulatory period of Indian Anthropology from 1774, he differed with his teacher as resards the year of beginning of the constructive period in Indian anthropology which began in 1920, instead of 1912 as argued by Majumdar. Vidyarthi pointed out that so many important constructive developments took place in Indian anthropology in and around 1920 and, therefore, 1920 should be considered as the beginning of this period. In order to support his arguments, Vidyarthi pointed out that for the first time in India, the teaching of anthropology was started in 1920 in the

University of Calcutta. The teaching of Sociology again for the first time was started in 1919 in the University of Bombay, in which social anthropology was also included and Vidyarthi further argued that, besides these two major developments, the publication of the first anthropological research journal MAN IN INDIA, was also started in 1921 by Sir S.C. Roy which coincides with two major achievements, as pointed out above. Thus according to Vidyarthi the constructive period in Indian anthropology began in 1920, which continued till India became free in 1947.

About the third phase in Indian anthropology, Vidyarthi did not approve the word "critical" as suggested by Majumdar, he rather argued to call the third phase as "Analytical" period, which began in Indian Anthropology after the second world war, especially when India got her independence. He is of the opinion that there was a positive increase in contacts with the American social anthropologists after India's independence, among whom special mention may be made of Morris Opler of the Cornell University (1948, 1950), Oscar Lewis of the University of Illinois (1951), David G. Mandelbaum of the University of California and Robert Redfield, Milton Singer, Mekim Marriott etc. of the University of Chicago, who not only stayed in India and conducted empirical field works, but they also created an atmosphere for analytical study of Indian villages, historical cities etc. with a view to testing certain hypotheses and to refine some of the methodological framework developed in America and elsewhere. Thus according to Vidyarthi this was an appropriate phase of development to be called as an analytical period in Indian Anthropology. During this period, which is still continuing, researches on tribes, castes, villages, urban cities of both orthogenetic and hetrogenetic (Redfield, 1956) nature etc. were attempted to by the Indian Anthropologists, trained in European and American Universities from the theoretical and methodological points of view. The beginning of this phase also coincides with the publication of Srinivas's book Religion and Society among the Coorgs of South India (1952), which marked a departure from the descriptive phase to an analytical one. Besides Srinivas's book, the publication of Iravati Karve's book Kinship

Organisation in India (1953) again reflected the beginning of a turning point in Indian Anthropology. Thus Vidyarthi seems to be quite justified in calling this phase of the Indian Anthropology an analytical one.

It is evident from the foregoing discussion that whatever theoretical contributions Indian Anthropologists have made to enrich the Indian Anthropology, have been made mainly during the last three decades, specially after the beginning of analytical period. For, during the last two periods of Indian Anthropology, the British Officers and some early ethnographers mainly concentrated on the "fact finding mission" rather making any substantial theoretical and methodological contributions to Indian Anthropology. Hence the discussions on various themes and concepts or the theoretical or methodological contributions of Indian anthropologists, will mainly confine to the works done or being done in the so-called analytical period (i.e. from 1950 onwards).

Great and Little Tradition

In studying a civilization Redfield (1897-1958) developed (1955, 56) his propositions of Great and Little Traditions. According to him the intellectual influences that come from outside the village may be termed as "Great tradition" and those coming from the local areas are termed as the "Little tradition". He also introduced the term "cultural specialists" for such organized groups of people as mediate between the great and little traditions. Redfield further introouced Milton Singer's concept of "cultural media" such as song, dance recitation etc., through which cultural specialists communicate to the masses and, thus, establish continuity between the two traditions.

Following the terms and concepts of Redfield, Miltoı Singer came to India (1954-55) and applied to his study o Indian Civilization some of the views and concepts of Redfield as stated above. He studied the city of Madras and cxamine the concepts of Redfield with special reference to cultura specialists on Indian situations and formulated some othe concepts such as cultural media, cultural performances, cultura stages etc.

Great tradition as developed by Redfield in 1956 refers to the formal, literate tradition of a civilization, which is maintained by the elite of the society. The great tradition contracts with the culture of the rural people of the same civilization, which he called little tradition. These concepts were proposed and elaborated by Redfield in his book Peasant Society and Culture (1956). Most of the discussions on great tradition have focused on the civilizations of the Near East and Asia especially India, but Redfield also applied this concept in the study of Maya Civilization, whose conquest by the Spanish, he viewed, as the removal of great tradition.

In the study of Indian civilization this concept has been applied and examined by several anthropologists—Vidyarthi 1961, Narayan 1969, Jha, 1971, Narayan, 1971, Mahapatra, 1972, Saraswati 1975, Narayan, 1978, Vidyarthi and Saraswati, 1978, Narayan, 1973, Narayan, 1984 (Basukinath). It has been modified also by Narayan (1971) and Saraswati (1975) who calls it Shastriya and Laukik tradition instead of great tradition as argued by Redfield. Little tradition refers to the culture of the rural village living within a civilization. The little tradition contrasts with the great tradition, which is the formal tradition of the civilization. After these concepts were published, Redfield became quite popular and now these concepts are usually identified with him.

Elements of the little tradition are continuously incorporated into the great tradition through a process of universalization. Likewise elements of the great tradition filter down to the village level, but in the process of parochialisation the elements are transformed, modified or reinterpreted to fit the rural peasant tradition. According to Redfield this concept of little tradition does not apply to primitive societies, whose culture is thought to be autonomous.

Sacred Complex

The anthropological approach to the study of civilization is a late comer in Indian Anthropology. Initiated by A.L. Kroeber, Ralph Linton, Robert Redfield, Milton Singer others in the fifties it was introduced in India by Nirmal Kumar Bose, Oravati Karve and L.P. Vidyarthi. The anthropological approach to the study of civilization is primarily based on the part-whole interactions within the civilizational frame. The Anthropologists relate some elements of the Great tradition to the life of the ordinary folk and rural people.

Since the publication of the SACRED COMPLEX of Hindu Gaya (1961), the various dimensions of Indian civilization have been studied by several scholars. During last twenty six years several studies have been undertaken which go a long way in establishing as well as refining the terms and concepts, methods and approaches to the study of Indian civilization.

Under the guidance of his teachers Robert Redfield and Milton Singer, Vidyarthi studied the sacred city of Gaya as a dimension of Indian civilization and indeed it was a beginning of an anthropological approach to study places of pilgrimage as civilization centres, Vidyarthi took sometime to refine and modify several analytical concepts, which are now in vogue in the study of Indian civilization.

In the study of the sacred complex of Hindu Gaya (1961) several terms were used by Vidyarthi such as 'Sacred cluster', 'Sacred segment' and 'Sacred zone' to describe the Sacred centres constituting the sacred Geography of Gaya, Local, Regional and Universal, to indicate the scope of some of the elements of the sacred complex, and Folk, Sanskritic, Feudalistic and proletarian to describe the nature of priesthood. These terms provided a typology for describing the patterns of a sacred complex,

The main finding of Gaya, thus, was that the sacred complex in Hindu Gaya is based on trichotomic interrelated phenomena viz. The Sacred Geography', The 'Sacred performances' and The 'Sacred Specialists', The Complex network of relationship which connects Hindu Gaya with other centres and regions of India, was also brought to light. Finally on the basis of these three analytical concepts, as referred to above, Vidyarthi said "these three concepts ; conceived collectively, are termed as sacred complex" (1961, pp. 113).

While Vidyarthi developed the concept of Sacred Complex for studying the places of pilgrimage as a dimension of Indian civilization, Marriott and Bernard S. Cohn developed the concepts of "Network and centres" (1958) to study the channels of integration of Indian civilization, wherein they discussed the similar theme conceptually. Thus, in Indian anthropology, the concepts of "sacred complex" and "Network and centres" have become very popular theoretically as model for studying the traditional cities and places of pilgrimage as a dimension of Indian civilization.

Criticism

No watertight compartment can be made between the Sacred and Secular ; rather there is continuity.

Other major works in Sacred Complex :—

Narayan, Rajgir—1969

Narayan, Deoghar—1971

M. Jha, Janakpur—1971

Mahapatra, Lingraj temple

Bhubneswar—1972

Saraswati Holy circuit of

Nimsar—1965

Morab and Goswami—Chamundeshwar

temple (Mysore)—1975

P. Chakravarty—Tarkeshwar

Temple in West Bengal—1975

Narayan—Bodh Gaya—1978

Vidyarthi & Saraswati Kashi—1978

Narayan, Deoghar and Rajgir—1983

Narayan—Basukinath- 1984 (March)

Universalisaton and Parochialisation

Being a disciple of Redfield, Mekim Marriott applied some of the concepts of Redfield in the context of Indian villages which he studied as part of the Complex Indian Social System. Marriott studied a village in U.P. known as Kishangarhi (1955) and later on he organised a seminar at Chicago on village India, which came out in a book form in 1955 under the editorship of Marriott. Thus, Marriott while studying the Indian Village modified the great and little traditions as developed earlier by Redfield, and argued tnat the twin concepts of "Universalization" and 'Parochialisation' are operating in the socio-religious systems of Indian Villages. According to Marriott the concept of 'Universalization' refers to the "Carrying forward of materials which are already present in the little traditions which it compasses" (1955). The opposite process, that of parochialisation, is defined by him as the "downward devolution of great traditional elements and their integration with little traditional elements. It is a process of localisation".

Thus Marriott has perceptively christened two contrasting, yet, complementary process of cultural growth of the indigenous civilization in India as Universalisation and Parochialisation. He is of the opinion that "an indigenous civilization is one whose great traditions originate by Universalization", while these great traditions are localised by parochialisation as put forward by Marriott.

Finally Meckim Marriott pointed out that these processes are by their nature, not restricted to the Hindu culture, but are applicable to all cultures having the dimensions of the Great and Little traditions.

Another alumni of the Chicago School of Anthropology Milton Singer tried to understand the processes, unity and continuity of Indian Civilization (1958, 1964, 1972). Following A.L Kroeber and Robert Redfield, Milton Singer conceives Indian civilization "as a coherent structure of rural network and urban centres which at the same time acts as a medium for the mutual communication of great and little traditions and of other cultural differences between and among tribes and castes, linguistic regions, and centres, town and country (964 p. 110). In order to comprehend the process of growth and spread of a "primary Civilization" like that of India, Singer attaches importance to a study of the encounters between primary Civilizations and the alien pre-civilized or civilized cultures, by understanding detailed investigation of the institutions, specialists and media, of which a civilization makes use for the transmission of cultural traditions.

Tribe-Caste Continuum

Although the concept of "Continuum" owes its origin to Redfield (1957) when he published The Folk Culture of Yucatan (1941), but in Indian anthropology the problem of tribe-caste continuum has attracted the attention of Indian Ethnographers and Census Commissioners of India who faced difficulties indicating where the category of "tribe" ended and "caste" began. Risley pointed out (1891, 1915) that it was difficult to "draw a demarcating line between tribe and caste". F.G. Bailey (1960,61), however, presented a more systematic interactional mode for considering the position of the tribe vis-a-vis caste as two ideal poles in a linear continuum. He argued that whereas the tribe is typically organised on the basis of segementry solidarity, the caste system is based on organic solidarity (Bailey. Ibid).

However, taking off from Bailey's interpretation of continuum, Surjit Sinha, a disciple of Robert Redfield, examined the Enthnographic materials of the Bhumij from Birbhum and some of the tribes of Bastar (1965) (1957-1965) and suggested that the continuum be conceived simultaneously and yet distinctively on the level of social structure and culture, both as ethnic groups and as local communities. Following Surjit Sinha's theoretical outline H.N. Banerjee (1969) has made a detailed study of the pattern of tribe caste continuum among the Korwa of Manabhum.

Surjit Sinha is of the opinion that "Many of the lower castes in India seem to share with the tribals the following characteristics : emphasis on equality in social behaviour within one's ethnic group, considerable freedom of cultural participation for the women, and a value system little burdened by puritanical asceticism, further, the supernaturalism of these lowest castes has some similarities with that of tribes in that their pantheon primarily consist of local gods, while their supernaturalism is rarely accompanied by ethnical considerationas" (Sinha : 1978).

Elaborating his view on "Rajputisation" of tribes in central India, Surjit Sinha has argued that state formation in the tribal belt of central Indian is very largely a story of Rajputisation of the tribes" (1978, p. 5). He further says "the diffusion of the Rajput model of state as also the indigenous developmental processes could gain ground only among those tribal groups who had attained the technological level of settled agriculture" (Ibid).

He pointed out that the most striking and important impact of state formation on the international structure of these tribes was, of course, the stratification of the hitherto equalitarian society into social classes. Social stratification follows mainly the lines of sub-infeudation of territorial units. On the whole, power, economy and social status have a fairly close correlation in the regional system of stratification. However, the final validation of a status is in terms of kinship (fictitious or real), marriage alliance and ritual symbols. A poor person related by kinship and marriage to wealthy Rajput family gains considerable prestige from the right kinds of symbolic association with the caste status of the Rajput. In other words, there is a hierarchic structural and ideological (or mythical) link between the ordinary tribals of central India and the Rajputs of the highest order in North Western India. The myth of the Rajput standard of living and the structural framework of states ruled by Rajput and pseudo-Rajput lineage of various orders connects the tribal belt of the central India in a special way to the mainstream of Hindu civilization and thereby establishes a very strong tribe-caste continuum, which needs a detailed study in historical and functional perspectives.

Again, at the contextual level, the study of tribe caste continuum, made by Sachchidanand (1970, p. 165; pp. 173-997) with special reference to the Gonds of Bihar is also significant. Narayan's study of Kheturi (1984) in the context of tribe caste continuum is also significant.

This concept of tribe-caste continuum may also be elaborated at the textual level. The reference of various tribes like Khasi, Kirant, Bhils etc. in our Epics like the Ramayan, the Mahabharat, the Kirata Arjun and various Purans like the Vayu Puran, the Vishnu Puran etc. when the tribal cults have been universalised to a great level of elaboration reveal as to how the little tradition of tribal India have contributed and enriched the rise and development of Indian Civilization.

Among the scholars, who have made significant contributions to this concept, special mention may be made of

N.K. Bose, Martin Orans and others. As early as in 1949, Bose argued that the tribes are being pulled towards the caste system mainly through agriculture and craft based economy of the caste society, His paper Hindu methods of Tribal absorption (1941, 1953) reveals as to how most primitive tribe like the Juang (of Orissa) had been influenced by the Brahmanical influence, although they are living outside the pale of Hinduism since time immemorial as observed by the author as early as January 1928. Martin Orans, in his famous book SANTAL—A TRIBE IN SEARCH OF A GREAT TRADITION (1965) has emphasised that how a tribe has been looking towards the great traditional elements of high Hinduism, which has pulled the tribe towards emulating the caste pattern.

Dominant Caste

After the publication of Srinivas's paper on Dominant Caste in Rampura in American Anthropologist (1959, Vol 61), the concept of dominant caste attracted the attention of Indian anthropologists and sociologists among whom special mention may be made of S.C. Dubey (1961) and B.K. Roy Burman (1978), who have disagreed with Srinivas over the use and existence of the dominant caste. Dubey in his critical essay argued that, instead of any caste group, an individual dominates in the society. He expressed difficulties in using this concept is a conctete field situation. Dubey also pointed out that the political power remained concentrated in a few individuals rather than diffused in caste. Arguing over the concept of Dominant Caste B.K. Roy Burman (1978) has pointed out that instead of dominants for individuals, there are dominant communities which may have several dimensions viz. control over economic resources, control over social status, maintenance of law etc. In this way Srinivas's concepts of Dominant Caste has attracted the attention of scholars in Indian anthr opology and sociology.

2

TRIBALS OF INDIA

Tribe

Generally speaking by the term 'tribe' we mean a group of people living at a particular place from the time immemorial.

Anthropologically the tribe is a system of social organisation which includes several local groups—villages, bands, districts or lineages- and normally include a common territory, a common language and a common culture. The elements constituting the tribe may or may not be coordinated by formal or centralized political power, ideally the term tribe implies large element of solidarity based on strongly shared primary sentiments. Such solidarity becomes contractual in nature as the tribal organization becomes more formally organised. The point at which these latter characteristics become pronounced is, perhaps, a convenient place to distinguish between the tribe and the nation. In general, anthropologists agree on the criteria by which a tribe may be described : common territory, a tradition of common descent, common language, common culture, a common name, political system, simple economy, religion and belief, primitive law and own educational system.

A scheduled tribe is he who has been mentioned in the scheduled list of the Indian Constitution under article 342 (i) and 342 (ii). According to article 342 (i) The President may with respect to any state, and where it is state specified in part A or part B of the first schedule, after consultation with the Governor or Rajpramukh thereof, by public notification, specify the tribes or tribal communities or parts or groups within tribes or tribal communities or parts or groups within tribes or tribal communities which shall for the purpose of this constitution be deemed to be the scheduled tribes in relation to that state.

According to article 342(2) parliament may by law include in or exclude from the list of scheduled Tribes specified in a notification issued under clause (1) any tribe or tribal community or part or group within any tribe or tribal community but save as aforesaid a notification issued under the said clause shall not be varied by any subsequent notification. According to 1981 census there are 559 scheduled tribes and 1087 scheduled castes in India. The statewise distribution is as follows :—

State	Total No. of Scheduled castes	Total No. of Scheduled Tribes
Andhra Pradesh	59	33
Assam	16	14
Bihar	23	30
Gujarat	30	29
Haryana	37	—
Himachal Pradesh	56	08
Jammu & Kashmir	13	—
Karnataka	101	49
Kerala	68	35
Madhya Pradesh	47	46
Maharashtra	59	47
Manipur	07	29
Nagaland	—	05
Orissa	93	62
Punjab	37	—
Rajasthan	59	12

State	Total No. of Scheduled castes	Total No. of Scheduled Tribes
Sikkim	04	02
Tamil Nadu	76	36
Tripura	32	19
Uttar Pradesh	66	05
West Bengal	59	38
Andaman and Nicobar Islands	—	06
Arunachal Pradesh	16	12
Chandigarh	36	—
Dadar and Nagar Haveli	04	07
Delhi	36	—
Goa, Daman and Diu	—	02
Lakshadweep	—	02
Mizoram	16	14
Pondicherry	15	—
Total:	1087	559

STATEMENT 1

Ranking of states and union territories by population size

Rank in 1981	States/Union Territories in order of Population size	Population in 1981	Percentage to total population of India 1981	Rank in 1971	Population in 1971
1	2	3	4	5	6
	INDIA@	685,184,692	100.00		548,159,652
1	Uttar Pradesh	110,862,013	16.18	1	88,341,144
2	Bihar	69,914,734	10.20	2	56,353,369

1	2	3	4	5	6
3	Maharashtra	62,784,171	9.16	3	50,412,235
4	West Bengal	54,580,647	7.97	4	44,312,011
5	Andhra Pradesh	53,549,673	7.82	5	43,502,708
6	Madhya Pradesh	62,178,844	7.62	6	41,654,119
7	Tamil Nadu	48,408,077	7.06	7	41,199,168
8	Karnataka	37,115,714	5.42	8	29,299,168
9	Rajasthan	34,261,826	5.00	9	25,765,806
10	Gujarat	34,085,799	4.97	10	26,697,475
11	Orissa	26,370,271	3.85	11	21,844,615
12	Kerala	25,453,680	3.71	12	21,347,375
13	Assam	19,836,843	2.90	13	14,625,152
14	Punjab	16,788,915	2.45	14	13,551,060
15	Haryana	12,922,618	1.89	15	10,036,808
16	Delhi	6,220,406	0.91	17	4,065,698
17	Jammu & Kashmir @	5,987,389	0.87	16	4,616,632
18	Himachal Pradesh	4,280,818	0.62	18	3,460,434
19	Tripura	2,053,058	0.30	19	1,556,342
20	Manipur	1,420,953	0.21	20	1,072,753
21	Meghalaya	1,336,819	0.19	21	1,011,699
22	Goa, Daman & Diu	1,086,730	0.16	22	857,771
23	Nagaland	774,930	0.11	23	516,449
24	Arunachal Pradesh	631,839	0.09	25	467,511
25	Pondicherry	604,471	0.09	24	471,707
26	Mizoram	433,757	0.07	26	332,390
27	Chandigarh	451,610	0.07	27	257,251

28	Sikkim	316,385	2.05	28	202,843
29	Andaman & Nicobar Islands	188,741	0.03	29	115,133
30	Dadra & Nagar Haveli	103,676	0.02	30	74,170
31	Lakshadweep	40,249	0.01	31	31,810

*Projected.

@Excludes the population of areas under unlawful occupation of Pakistan and China where census could not be taken.

Uttar Pradesh continues to retain its first position. Most of the other states have continued to retain their original ranks. Rajasthan has overtaken Gujarat and has moved up from 10th place in 1971 to the 9th place in 1981, while Gujarat has moved from the 9th place in 1971 to the 10th place in 1981. Delhi which was 17th in rank in 1971 has overtaken Jammu & Kashmir and moved to the 16th place in 1981, while Jammu & Kashmir has moved from the place in 1971 to the 17th place in 1981.

Statement 2 gives the proportion of scheduled tribes to total population as enumerated at the 1971 and 1981 censuses along with the absolute figures.

The figures reveal that the proportion of scheduled tribes to total population in India was 6.82 percent according to 1971 census. It has slightly gone up to 7.76 percent in 1981. The same position prevailed in 1971 census also.

Among States, Nagaland occupies the first place having 83.99% followed by Meghalaya 80.58%. Among union territories the proportions are quite high in case of Arunachal Pradesh (69.82%), Dadra & Nagar Haveli (78.82), Lakshadweep (93.82%) and Mizoram (93.55%) which are predominantly populated by tribal population.

STATEMENT 2

Percentage of scheduled tribes to total population by sex for state/union territory as enumerated at the 1971 and 1981 censuses

India/State/ Union Territory	Persons males Females	Total population	1971 Total scheduled tribes population	1971 Percentage of scheduled tribes population to total population	1981 Total population	1981 Total Scheduled tribes population	1981 Percentage of scheduled tribes population to total population
1	2	3	4	5	6	7	8
INDIA @	P	533,534,500	36,408,514	6.82	665,287,849	51,628,638	7.76
	M	276,335,036	18,361,797	6.64	343,930,423	26,038,535	7.57
	F	257,199,464	18,046,717	7.02	321,357,426	25,590,103	7.96
STATES							
1 Andhra Pradesh	P	43,502,708	1,657,657	3.81	53,549,673	3,176,001	5.93
	M	22,008,663	840,022	3.82	27,108,922	1,618,689	5.97
	F	21,494,045	317,635	3.80	26,440,751	1,557,312	5.89

1	2	3	4	5	6	7	8
2 Bihar	P	56,353,369	4,932,767	8.75	69,914,734	5,810,867	8.31
	M	28,846,944	2,462,265	8.54	35,930,560	2,915,492	8.11
	F	27,506,425	2,470,502	8.98	33,984,174	2,895,375	8.52
3 Gujarat	P	26,697,475	3,734,422	13.99	34,085,799	4,848,586	14.22
	M	13,802,494	1,897,204	13.75	17,552,640	2,453,566	13.98
	F	12,894,981	1,837,218	14.25	16,533,159	2,395,020	14.49
4 Haryana	P	10,036,808	...	...	12,922,618	...	...
	M	5,377,258	...	...	6,909,938	...	...
	F	4,659,550	...	...	6,012,680	...	...
5 Himachal Pradesh	P	3,460,434	141,610	4.09	4,280,818	197,263	4.61
	M	1,766,957	70,810	4.01	2,169,931	99,727	4.60
	F	1,693,477	70,800	4.18	2,110,887	97,536	4.62
6 Jammu & Kashmir @	P	4,616,632	...	...	5,987,389	...	...
	M	2,458,315	...	...	3,164,660	...	...
	F	2,158 317	...	...	2,822,729	...	...
7 Karnataka	P	29,299,014	231,268	0.79	37,135,714	1,825,203	4.91
	M	14,971,900	118,203	0.79	18,922,627	926,235	4.89
	F	14,327,114	113,065	0.79	18,213,087	898,968	4.94

1	2	3	4	5	6	7	8
8 Kerala	P	21,347,375	269,356	1.26	25,453,680	261,475	1.03
	M	10,587,851	134,996	1.28	12,527,767	131,243	1.05
	F	10,759,524	134,360	1.25	12,925,913	130,232	1.01
9 Madhya	P	41,654,119	8,387,403	20.14	52,178,844	11,987,031	22.97
Pradesh	M	21,455'334	4,198,509	19.57	26,886,305	6,003,304	22.33
	F	20,198,785	4,188,891	20.74	25,292,539	5,983,727	23.66
10 Maharashtra	P	50,412,235	2,954,249	5.86	62,784,171	5,772,038	9.19
	M	26,116,351	1,497,481	5.73	32,415,126	2,923,955	9 02
	F	24,295,884	1,456,768	6.00	30,369,045	2,848,083	9.38
11 Manipur	P	1,072,753	334,466	31.18	1,420,953	397,977	27.30
	M	541,675	166,490	30.74	721,006	196,455	27.25
	F	531,078	167,976	31.63	699,947	191,522	27.36
12 Meghalaya	P	1,011,699	814,230	80.48	1,335,819	1,076,345	80.58
	M	520,967	407,859	78.29	683,710	537,635	78.63
	F	490,732	406,371	82.81	652,109	438,710	82.61
13 Nagaland	P	516,449	457,602	88.61	774,930	650.885	83.99
	M	276,084	231,921	84.00	415,910	332,943	80.05
	F	240,365	225,681	93.89	359,020	317,942	88.56

1	2	3	4	5	6	7	8
14 Orissa	P	21,944,615	5,071,937	23.11	26,370,271	5,915,067	22.43
	M	11,041,083	2,526,663	22.88	13,309,786	2,939,863	22.09
	F	10,903,532	2,545,274	23.34	13,060,485	2,975,204	22.78
15 Punjab	P	13,551,060	...	...	16,788,915	...	...
	M	7,266,515	...	...	8,937,210	...	...
	F	6,284,545	...	...	7,851,705	...	...
16 Rajasthan	P	25,765,806	3,125,506	12.13	34,261,862	4,183,124	12.21
	M	13,484,383	1,619,210	12.01	17,854,154	2,150,767	12.05
	F	12,281,423	1,506,296	12.26	16,407,708	2,032,357	12.39
17 Sikkim	P	209,843	...	...	316,3	73,623	23.27
	M	112,662	...	...	172,440	38,211	22.16
	F	97,181	...	...	143,945	35,412	24.60
18 Tamil Nadu	P	41,199,168	311,515	0.76	48,408,077	550,226	1.07
	M	20,828,021	159,706	0.77	24,487,624	264,288	1.08
	F	20,371,147	151,809	0.75	23,920,453	255,938	1.07
19 Tripura	P	1,556,342	450,544	28.95	2,053,058	583,920	28.44
	M	801,126	230,544	28.78	1,054,846	297,612	28.21
	F	755,216	220,000	29.13	998,212	286,308	28.68

	1	2	3	4	5	6	7	8
20	Uttar Pardesh	P	88,341,144	198,565	0.22	110,862,013	232,705	0.21
		M	47,016,421	105,608	0.22	58,819,276	121,508	0.21
		F	41,324,723	92,957	0.22	52,042,737	111,199	0.21
21	West Bengal	P	44,312,011	2,532,969	5.72	54,580,647	3,070,672	5.63
		M	23,435,987	1,295,460	5.53	28,560,901	1,559,288	5.46
		F	20,876,024	1,237,509	5.93	26,019,746	1,511,384	5.81
	UNION TERRITORIES							
1	Andaman & Nicobar Islands	P	115,133	18,102	15.72	188,741	22,361	11.85
		M	70,027	9,320	13.31	107,261	11,586	10.80
		F	45,106	8,782	19.47	81,480	10,775	13.22
2	Arunachal Pradesh	P	467,511	369,408	79.02	631,839	441,167	69.82
		M	251,231	184,076	73.27	339,322	220,046	64.85
		F	216,280	185,332	85.69	292,517	221,121	75.59
3	Chandigarh	P	257,251	...	...	451,610	...	...
		M	147,080	...	...	255,278	...	...
		F	110,171	...	...	196,332	...	...
4	Dadra & Nagar Haveli	P	74,170	64,445	88.89	103,676	81,714	78.82
		M	36,964	31,985	85.53	52,515	40,486	77.09
		F	37,206	32,460	87.24	51,161	41,228	80.58

1	2	3	4	5	6	7	8
5 Delhi	P	4,065,698	...	...	6,220,406	...	...
	M	2,257,515	...	...	3,440,081	...	...
	F	1,808,183	...	...	2,780,325	...	...
6 Goa, Daman, & Diu	P	857,771	7,654	0.89	1,086,730	10,721	0.99
	M	431,214	3,836	0.89	548,450	5,512	1.01
	F	426,557	3,818	0.90	538,280	5,209	0.97
7 Lakshadweep	P	31,810	29,540	92.86	40,249	37,760	93.82
	M	16,078	14,614	90.89	20.377	18,865	92.53
	F	15,732	14,926	94.88	19,872	18,895	95.08
8 Mizoram	P	332,390	313,299	94.26	493,757	461,907	93.55
	M	170,824	155,015	90.75	257,239	231,261	89.90
	F	161,566	158,284	97.97	236.518	230,646	97.52
9 Pondicherrry	P	471,707	...	...	604,471	...	...
	M	237,112	...	...	304,561	...	...
	F	234,595	...	...	299,910	...	...

NOTES

(1) *Excludes Assam where census could not be held owing to disturbed conditions prevailing there at the time of 1981 census. 1971 census figures also exclude Assam to make the date comparable. The population figures of India including the population of Assam and Assam separately for 1971 are as follows ;

	Persons Males Females	1971 Total population	Total scheduled tribes population	Percentage of scheduled tribes population to total population
INDIA	P	548,159,652	38,015,162	6.94
	M	284,049,276	19,181,450	6.75
	F	264,110,376	18,833,712	7.13
Assam	P	14,625,152	1,606.648	10.99
	M	7,714,240	819,653	10.63
	F	6,910,912	786,995	11.39

(2) @Excludes the population of areas under unlawful occupation of Pakistan and China where censu s could not be taken.

(3) †This figure would appear to include high returns relating to certain communities with nomen clatures similar to those included in the list of scheduled tribes consequent on the removal of area restrictions.

(4) † Please see also the foot note at 3 relating to Karnataka State.

(5) No tribes were scheduled by the President of india for Haryana Jammu & Kashmir, Punjab, Chandigarh, Delhi and Pondicherry.

(6) No tribes were scheduled under the Constitution in relation to Sikkim in 1971 census under the Representation for Sikkim Subject Regulation (1966).

(7) 1971 figures of Scheduled Tribes are the enumerated figures based on Scheduled Castes and Scheduled Tribes Lists (Modificaon) Order, 1956 and other relevant Acts and Orders. 1981 figures of Scheduled Tribes are the enumerated figures based on Scheduled Castes and Scheduled Tribes orders (Amendment) Act, 1976 and other relevant Acts and Orders.

Statement 3 gives the percentage distribution of scheduled tribes to total population in India, states and union territories by total, rural and urban. It also furnishes the percentage distribution of members of scheduled tribes of India. The percentage of scheduled tribes population to all population in rural and urban areas are 9.54 and 2.03 percent respectively. In rural areas it is the highest in Lakshadweep (96.61%) followed by Mizoram (95.02%). Among the states, Meghalaya and Nagaland are predominatly tribal areas, having the percentage of 86.13 and 89.70 respectively. In the case of urban areas the highest percentage is again found in the union territory of Lakshadweep (90.57%) followed by Mizoram (89.05%). Among the states, the percentages are again high in the states of Meghalaya (53.36%)and Nagaland (52.91%). Percentages of Scheduled Tribes in this statement and subsequent statements in respect of Karnataka and India for 1981 census are derived from the absolute figures given in the Primary Census Abstract which may please be read along with foot notes No. 2 and 4 thereof.

STATEMENT 3

Percentage of members of scheduled tribes population in total, rural and urban areas in states/Union territories, 1981

India/State/ Union Territory	Percentage of Scheduled Tribes to									Distribution of 100 members of scheduled tribes among state/union territory
	Total			Rural			Urban			
	P	M	F	P	M	F	P	M	F	
1	2	3	4	5	6	7	8	9	10	11
INDIA	7.76	7.57	7.96	9.54	9.37	9.72	2.03	2.00	2.07	100.00
STATES :										
1 Andhra Pradesh	5.93	5.97	5.89	7.25	7.32	7.19	1 58	1 62	1.54	6.15
2 Bihar	8.31	8.11	8.52	8.90	8.74	9.07	4.15	3.99	4.35	11.26
3 Gujarat	14.22	13.98	14.49	19.13	18.91	19.37	3.35	3.37	3.33	9.39
4 Himachal Pradesh	4.61	4.60	4.62	4.91	4.93	4.89	0.96	0.99	0.91	0.38

1	2	3	4	5	6	7	8	9	10	11
5 Karnataka	4.91	4.89	4.94	6.02	6.03	6.01	2.19	2.16	2.22	3.54
6 Kerala	1.03	1.05	1.01	1.24	1.27	1.22	0.10	0.11	0.10	0.51
7 Madhya Pradesh	22.97	22.33	23.66	27.78	27.15	28.44	4.10	4.10	4.10	23.22
8 Maharashtra	9.19	9.02	9.38	12.67	12.71	12.74	2.74	2.65	2.84	11.18
9 Manipur	27.30	27.25	27.36	32.79	32.71	32.87	12.03	12.05	12.01	0.75
10 Meghalaya	80 58	78.63	82.61	86.13	84.92	87.40	55.36	51.03	60.16	2.09
11 Nagaland	83.99	80.05	80.56	89.70	86.76	92.97	52.91	47.58	60.65	1,26
12 Orissa	22.43	22.09	.78	24.26	24.06	24.46	8.77	8.37	9.23	11.46
13 Rajasthan	12.21	12.05	12.39	14.89	14.72	15.06	2.16	2.27	2.04	8.10
14 Sikkim	23.27	22.16	24.60	23.60	22.75	24.59	21.54	19.35	24.67	0.14
15 Tamil Nadu	1.07	1.08	1.07	1.45	1.46	1.43	0.32	0.31	0.32	1.01
16 Tripura	28.44	28.21	28.68	31.53	31.24	31.85	3.40	3.59	3.20	1.13
17 Uttar Pradesh	0.21	0.21	0.21	0.24	0.24	0.25	0.06	0.06	0.05	0.45
18 West Bengal	5.63	5.46	5.81	7.36	7.26	7.47	0,80	0.78	0,82	5.95

1	2	3	4	5	6	7	8	9	10	11
UNION TERRITORIES :										
1 Andaman & Nicobar Islands	11.85	10.80	13.22	15.88	14.52	17.63	0.55	0.69	0.35	0 04
2 Arunachal Pradesh	69.82	64.85	75.59	73.02	68.33	78.34	24.28	21.92	28.03	0.85
3 Dadra & Nagar Haveli	78.82	77.09	80.58	81.57	79.97	83.20	40.30	38.76	42.03	0.16
4 Goa, Daman & Diu	0.99	1.01	0.97	1.12	1.16	1.08	0.71	0.70	0.71	0.02
5 Lakshadweep	93.82	92.58	95.08	96.61	95.71	97.52	90.57	88.99	92.22	0.07
6 Mizoram	93.55	89.90	97.52	95.02	91.92	98.36	89.05	83.84	94.88	0.89

Notes :

(1) *Excludes Assam where census could not be held owing to disturbed conditions prevailing there at the time of 1981 Census.

(2) No tribes were scheduled by the President of India for Haryana, Jammu & Kashmir, Punjab, Chandigarh, Delhi and Pondicherry.

Statement 4 gives the percentage distribution of total scheduled tribes population in India/State/Union Territory into rural and urban areas. The statement reveals that the percentage of scheduled tribes in rural areas is quite high in almost all states and union territories. The percentage of scheduled tribes in the urban areas is the highest in the union territory of Lakshadweep (44.68%) followed by Mizoram (23.48%). Among the states, Sikkim tops the list having 14.94% of scheduled tribes in urban areas followed by Karnataka (12.87%).

STATEMENT 4

Statement showing the percentage distribution of members of scheduled tribes in rural and urban areas to the total population of scheduled tribes, 1981

India/State/Union Territory	Percentage of Scheduled Tribes								
	Total			Rural			Urban		
	P	M	F	P	M	F	P	M	F
1	2	3	4	5	6	7	8	9	10
INDIA*	100.00	100.00	100.00	93.80	93.57	94.03	6.20	6.48	5.97
STATES :									
1. Andhra Pradesh	100.00	100.00	100.00	93.78	93.59	93.99	6.22	6.41	6.01
2. Bihar	100.00	100.00	100.00	93.77	93.49	94.05	6.23	6.51	5.95
3. Gujarat	100.00	100.00	100.00	92.68	92.36	93.00	7.32	7.64	7.00
4. Himachal Pradesh	100.00	100.00	100.00	98.42	98.20	98.65	1.58	1.80	1.35
5. Karnataka	100.00	100.00	100.00	87.13	86.99	87.29	12.87	13.01	12.71
6. Kerala	100.00	100.00	100.00	98.09	98.04	98.14	1.91	1.96	1.86
7. Madhya Pradesh	100.00	100.00	100.00	96.38	96.16	96.59	3.62	3.84	3.41
8. Maharshtra	100.00	100.00	100.00	89.57	89.24	89.91	10.43	10.76	10.09
9. Manipur	100.00	100.00	100.00	88.36	88.31	88.41	11.64	11.69	11.59

1	2	3	4	5	6	7	8	9	10
10. Meghalaya	100.00	100.00	100.00	87.59	87.97	87.20	12.41	12.03	12.80
11. Nagaland	100.00	100.00	100.00	90.23	89.82	90.65	9.77	10.18	9.35
12. Orissa	100.00	100.00	100.00	95.39	95.23	85.54	4.61	4.77	4.46
13. Rajasthan	100.00	100,00	100.00	96.27	95.94	86.62	3.73	4.06	3.38
14. Sikkim	100.00	100.00	100.00	85.06	84.76	85.28	14.94	16.24	14.62
15. Tamil Nadu	100.00	100.00	100.00	90.31	90.36	90.26	9.69	9.64	9.74
16. Tripura	100.00	100.00	100.00	93.69	98.61	98.77	1.31	1.39	1.23
17. Uttar Pradesh	100.00	100.00	100.00	95.28	95.02	95.57	4.72	4.98	4.43
18. West Bengal	100.00	100.00	100.00	96.24	96.03	96.46	3.76	3.97	3.54
UNION TERRITORIES :									
1. Andaman & Nicobar Islands	100.00	100.00	100.00	98.79	98.28	99.33	1.21	1.72	0.67
2. Arunachal Pradesh	100.00	100.00	100.00	97.72	97,47	97.97	2.28	2.53	2.03
3. Dadra & Nagar Haveli	100.00	100.00	100.00	96.59	96.49	96.69	3.41	3.51	3.31
4. Goa Daman & Diu	100.00	100.00	100.00	76.78	76.58	77.00	23.22	23.42	23.00
5. Lakshadweep	100.00	100.00	100.00	55.32	55.23	55.40	44.68	44.77	44.60
6. Mizoram	100.00	100.00	100.00	67.52	67.66	67.37	23.48	23.34	23.63

Notes :

1. *Excludes Assam where census could not be held owing to disturbed conditions prevailing there at the time of 1981 census.
2. No tribes were scheduled by the President of India for Haryana, Jammu & Kashmir, Punjab, Chandigarh, Delhi and Pondicherry.

Literates :

Columns 8 to 10 of the primary census abstract give the number of literate persons by sex among scheduled tribes. The definition of a literate person adopted in the 1981 census is as follows :—

> "A person who can both read and write with understanding in any language is to be taken as literate. A person who can merely read but cannot write, is not literate. It is not necessary that a person who is literate should have received any formal education or should have passed any minimum educational standard".

The test that was applied for reading was the ability to read any portion of the printed matter in the enumerator's instruction booklet (provided the person was familiar with the language used in the booklet) and the test for writing was the ability to write a simple letter. A child of the age of 4 years or less was treated as illiterate even if the child was going to a school and might have picked up reading and writing a few odd words.

Statement 5 gives the literacy rates among scheduled tribes in India, states and union territories. The literacy percentage among scheduled tribes in India works out to 16.35%. Among the states, Nagaland (40.32%) has the highest literacy rate followed by Manipur (39.74%). Among the union territories, the highest rank is occupied by Mizoram (59.63%) followed by Lakshadweep (53.13%). The same trend prevails in rural areas also.

In the case of urban areas the highest percentage of literates is found in Tripura (78.81%) followed by Nagaland (66.28%), among the states. Among the union territories, Mizoram occupies the highest position having the literacy rate of 74.04%.

STATEMENT 5

Literacy Rates in 1981

(The percentages of literates have been calculated on the total scheduled tribes population inclusive of the population in the age group 0-4)

India/State/Union Territory	Among the scheduled tribes total population			Among the scheduled tribes rural population			Among the scheduled tribes urban population		
	Persons	Males	Females	Persons	Males	Females	Persons	Males	Females
1	2	3	4	5	6	7	8	9	10
INDIA*	16.35	24.52	8.04	14.92	22.94	6.81	37.93	47.60	27.32
STATES :									
1. Andhra Pradesh	7.82	12.02	3.46	6.00	10.68	2.78	23.27	31.50	14.14
2. Bihar	16.99	26.17	7.75	15.56	24.63	6.48	38.53	48.30	27.78
3. Gujarat	21.14	30.41	11.64	20.34	29.53	11.00	31.27	41.16	20.20
4. Himachal Pradesh	25.93	38.75	12.82	25.40	38.21	12.36	59.15	68.61	46.19
5. Karnataka	20.14	29.96	10.03	17.94	27.60	8.03	35.00	45.72	23.70
6. Kerala	31.79	37.52	26.02	31.22	37.00	25.39	61.42	63.79	58.92

1	2	3	4	5	6	7	8	9	10
7. Madhya Pradesh	10.68	17.74	3.60	10.05	16.91	3.19	27.62	38.64	15.18
8. Maharashtra	22.29	32.38	11.94	19.35	29.18	9.34	47.55	58.90	35.12
9. Manipur	39.74	48.88	30.35	37.50	46.72	28.05	56.73	65.24	47.92
10. Meghalaya	31.55	34.19	28.91	27.09	29.76	24.39	63.03	66.60	59.68
11. Nagaland	40.32	47.32	32.99	37.50	44.59	30.15	66.28	71.36	60.50
12. Orissa	13.96	23.27	4.76	13.42	22.63	4.34	25.18	36.05	13.69
13. Rajasthan	10.27	18.85	1.20	9.61	17.88	0.93	27.31	41.93	8.70
14. Sikkim	33.13	43.10	22.37	29.14	39.44	18.09	55.84	63.43	47.32
15. Tamil Nadu	20.46	26.71	14.00	18.98	24.98	12.78	34.21	42.91	25.31
16. Tripura	23.07	33.46	12.27	22.33	32.74	11.52	78.81	84.42	72.21
17. Uttar Pradesh	20.45	31.22	8.69	18.96	29.66	7.33	69	60.92	38.12
18. West Bengal	13.21	21.16	5.01	12.72	20.69	4.53	72	32.36	18.02
UNION TERRITORIES :									
1. Andaman & Nicobar Islands	31.11	38.43	23.24	30.60	37.64	23.12	72.69	83.92	41.67
2. Arunachal Pradesh	14.04	20.79	7.31	13.23	19.76	6.78	43 39	60.63	33.18
3. Dadra & Nagar Haveli	16.86	25.46	8.42	16.32	24.76	8.00	32.34	44.87	19.28

1	2	3	4	5	6	7	8	9	10
4. Goa, Daman & Diu	26.48	33.65	18.89	26.24	33.00	19.12	27.28	35.79	18.11
5. Lakshadweep	53.13	63.	42.92	51.00	61.21	40.83	55.76	65.98	45.51
6. Mizoram	59.63	64.12	55.12	55.20	60.17	50.2I	74.04	77.11	71.01

Notes :

(1) *Excludes Assam where census could not be held owing to disturbed conditions prevailing there at the time of 1981 Census.

(2) No tribes were scheduled by the President of India for Haryana, Jammu & Kashmir, Punjab, Chandigarh, Delhi and Pondicherry.

Statement 6 gives the percentage distribution of population of scheduled tribes by sex into total workers, main workers, marginal workers and non-workers. The percentage of main workers to total scheduled tribes population works out to 42.54% for India. Among states it is the highest in Andhra Pradesh (49.39%). Among the union territories, Arunachal Pradesh (50.40%) has the highest percentage of main workers.

STATEMENT 6

Percentage distribution of scheduled tribes population of each sex into total workers, main workers, marginal workers & non-workers in states/union territories in 1981 census

India/State/Union Territory	Persons Males Females	Total Scheduled Tribes Population	Total Workers (Main+Marginal Workers)	Main Workers	Marginal Workers	Non-Workers
1	2	3	4	5	6	7
INDIA*	P	100.00	49.80	42.54	7.26	50.20
	M	100.00	58.13	56.66	1.47	41.87
	F	100 00	41.32	28.18	13.14	58.68
STATES						
1. Andhra Pradesh	P	100.00	53.95	49.39	4.57	46.04
	M	100.00	50.57	59.94	0.63	39.43
	F	100.00	47.09	38.43	8.66	52.91
2. Bihar	P	100.00	45.92	37.13	8.79	54.08
	M	100.00	57.03	54.92	2.11	42.97
	F	100.00	34.74	19.22	15.52	65.26

1	2	3	4	5	6	7
3. Gujarat	P	100.00	50.15	40.55	9.60	49.85
	M	100.00	57.03	56.85	0.88	42.27
	F	100.00	42.38	23.85	18.53	57.62
4. Himachal Pradesh	P	100.00	51.32	40.77	10.55	48.68
	M	100.00	57.10	53.64	3.46	42.90
	F	100.00	45.40	27.61	17.79	54.60
5. Karnataka	P	100.00	47.20	43.03	4.17	52.80
	M	100.00	58.48	57.78	0.70	41.52
	F	100.00	35.58	27.84	7.74	64.42
6. Kerala	P	100.00	45.25	40.53	4.72	54.75
	M	100.00	53.84	50.33	3.51	46.16
	F	100.00	36.60	30.66	5.94	63.40
7. Madhya Pradesh	P	100.00	53.35	46.28	7.07	46.65
	M	100.00	60.44	59.23	1.21	39.56
	F	100.00	46.24	33.29	12.95	53.76
8. Maharashtra	P	100.09	53.22	47.90	5.32	46.78
	M	100.00	58.29	56.77	1.52	41.71
	F	100.00	48.02	38.79	9.23	51.95

1	2	3	4	5	6	7
9. Manipur	P	100.00	48.93	47.87	1.06	51.07
	M	100.00	49.17	48.68	0.49	50.83
	F	100.00	48.67	47.04	1.63	51.33
10. Meghalaya	P	100.00	47.52	44.96	2.56	52.48
	M	100.00	53.04	52.09	0.95	46.96
	F	100.00	42.02	37.84	4.18	57.98

ANNEXE—2

List of Scheduled Castes and Scheduled Tribes

ANDHRA PRADESH

[The Scheduled Castes and Scheduled Tribes Orders (Amendment) Act, 1976 (No. 108 of 1976, dated the 18th September, 1976)]

SCHEDULED CASTES

1. Adi Andhra
2. Adi Dravida
3. Anamuk
4. Aray Mala
5. Arundhatiya
6. Arwa Mala
7. Bariki
8. Bavuri
9. Beda Jangam Budga Jangam
10. Bindla
11. Bygara
12. Ch hati
13. Chalavadi
14. Chamar, Mochi, Muchi
15. Chambhar
16. Chandala
17. Dakkal, Dokkalwar
18. Dandasi
19. Dhor
20. Dom, Dombara, Paidi, Pano
21. Ellamalawar, Yellammalawandlu
22. Ghasi, Handi, Relli Chachandi
23. Godagali
24. Godari
25. Gosangi
26. Holeya
27. Holeya Dasari
28. Jaggali
29. Jambuvulu
30. Kolupulvandlu
31. Madasi kuruva, Madari kuruve
32. Madiga
33. Madiga Dasu, Mashteen
34. Mahar
35. Mala
36. Mala Dasari
37. Mala Dasu
38. Mala Hannal

39. Malajangam
40. Mala Masti
41. Mala Sale, Netkaui
42. Mala Sanyasi
43. Mang
44. Mang Garodi
45. Manne
46. Mashti
47. Matangi
48. Mehtar
49. Mitha Ayyalvar
50. Mundala
51. Paky, Moti, Thoti
52. Pambada, Pambanda
53. Pamidi
54. Panchama, Pariah
55. Relli
56, Samagara
57. Samban
58. Sapru
59. Sindhollu, Chindollu

SCHEDULED TRIBES

1. Andh
2. Bagata
3. Bhil
4, Chenchu, Chenchwar
5. Gadabas
6. Gond, Naikpond, Rajgond
7. Goudu (in the Agency tracts)
8. Hill Reddis
9. Jatapus
10. Kammara
11. Kattunayakan
12. Kolam, Mannervarlu
13. Konda Dhoras
14. Konda Kapus
15. Kondareddis
16. Kondhs, Kodi, Kodhu, Desaya Kondhs, Dongria Kondhs, Kuttiya Kondhs, Tikiria Kondhs, Yenity Kondhs
17. Kotia, Bentho Oriya, Bartika, Dhulia, Dulia, Holva, Paiko, Putiya, Sanrona, Sidhopaink
18. Koya, Goud, Rajah, Rasha Koya, Lingadhari Koya (ordinary) Kottu Koya, Bhine Koya, Rajkoya
19. Kulia
20. Malis (excluding Adilabad, Hyderabad, Karimnagar, Khammam, Mahbubnagar, Medak, Nalgonda, Mamabad and Warangal districts)
21. Manna Dhora
22. Mukha Dhora, Nooka Dhora
23. Nayaks (in the Agency tracts)
24. Pardhan
25. Porja. Parangiperja
26. Reddi Dhoras
27. Rona, Rena
28. Savaras, Kapu Savaras Maliya Savaras, Khutto Savaras
29. Sugalis, Lambadis
30. Thoti (in Adilabad, Hyderabad, Karimnagar, Knammam, Mahbubnagar, Medak, Nalgonda, Nizamabad and Warangal districts)
31. Valmiki (in the Agency tracts)
32. Yenadis
33. Yerukulas

ASSAM

[The Scheduled Castes and Scheduled Tribes Orders (Amendment) Act, 1976 (No. 108 of 1976, dated the 18th September, 1976)]

SCHEDULED CASTES

1. Bansphor
2. Bhuinmali, Mali
3. Brittial Bania, Bania
4. Dhupi, Dhobi
5. Dugla, Dholi
6. Hira
7. Jalkeot
8. Jhalo, Malo, Jhalo-Malo
9. Kaibartta, Jaliya
10. Lalbegi
11. Mahara
12. Mehtar, Bhangi
13. Muchi, Rishi
14. Namasudra
15. Patni
16. Sutradhar

SCHEDULED TRIBES

1. In the autonomous districts :
   1. Chakma
   2. Dimasa, Kachari
   3. Garo
   4. Hajong
   5. Hmar
   6. Khasi, Jaintia, Synteng, Pnar War, Bhoi, Lyngngam
   7. Any Kuki Tribes, including :
      - (i) Biate, Biete
      - (ii) Changsan
      - (iii) Chongloi
      - (iv) Doungel
      - (v) Gamalhou
      - (vi) Gangte
      - (vii) Guite
      - (viii) Hanneng
      - (ix) Haokip, Haupit
      - (x) Haolai
      - (xi) Hengna
      - (xii) Hongsungh
      - (xiii) Hrangkhwal, Rangkhol
      - (xiv) Jongbe
      - (xv) Khawchung
      - (xvi) Rhawathlang, Khothalong
      - (xvii) Khelma
      - (xviii) Kholhou
      - (xix) Kipgen
      - (xx) Kuki
      - (xxi) Lengthang
      - (xxii) Lhangum
      - (xxiii) Lhoujem
      - (xxiv) Lhouvun
      - (xxv) Lupheng
      - (xxvi) Mangjel
      - (xxvii) Misao
      - (xxviii) Riang
      - (xxix) Sairhem
      - (xxx) Selnam
      - (xxxi) Singson
      - (xxxii) Sitlhou
      - (xxxiii) Sukte
      - (xxxiv) Thado
      - (xxxv) Thangngen
      - (xxxvi) Uibuh
      - (xxxvii) Vaiphei
   8. Lakher
   9. Man (Tai speaking)
   10. Any Mizo (Lushal) tribes
   11. Mikir
   12. Any Naga Tribes
   13. Pawi

14. Synteng

2. In the State of Assam excluding the autonomous districts :
   1. Barmans in Cachar
   2. Boro, Borokachari
   3. Deori
   4. Kachari. Sonwal
   5. Hojai
   6. Lalung
   7. Mech
   8. Miri
   9. Rabha

BIHAR

[The Scheduled Castes and Scheduled Tribes Orders (Amendment) Act, 1976 (No. 108 of 1976, dated the 18th September, 1976)]

SCHEDULED CASTES

1. Bauar
2. Bauri
3. Bhogta
4. Bhuiya
5. Bhumij (excluding North Chotanagpur and South Chotanagpur divisions and Santal Parganas district)
6. Chamar, Mochi
7. Chaupal
8. Dabgar
9. Dhobi
10. Dom, Dhanged
11. Dusadh, Dhari, Dharhi
12. Ghasi
13. Halalkhor
14. Hari, Mehtar, Bhangi
15. Kanjar
16. Kurariar
17. Lalbegi
18. Musahar
19. Nat
20. Pan, Sawasi
21. Pasi
22. Rajwar
23. Turi

SCHEDULED TRIBES

1. Asur
2. Baiga
3. Banjara
4. Bathudi
5. Bedia
6. Bhumij (in North Chotanagpur and South Chotanagpur divisions and Santal Parganas district)
7. Binjhia
8. Birhor
9. Birjia
10. Chero
11. Chik Baraik
12. Gond
13. Gorait
14. Ho
15. Karmali
16. Kharia
17. Kharwar
18. Khond
19. Kisan
20. Kora
21. Korwa
22. Lohara, Lohra
23. Mahli
24. Mal Paharia
25. Munda
26. Oraon
27. Parhaiya
28. Santal
29. Sauria Paharia
30. Savar

GUJARAT

[The Scheduled Castes and Scheduled Tribes Orders (Amendment) Act, 1976 (No. 108 of 1976, dated the 18th September, 1976)]

SCHEDULED CASTES

1. Ager
2. Bakad, Bant
3. Bawa-Dedh, Dedh-Sadhu
4. Bhambi, Bhambhi, Asadaru, Asodi, Chamadia, Chamar, Chambhar, Chamgar, Haralayya, Harali, Khalpa, Machigar, Mochigar, Madar, Madig Mochi, Nalia, Telegu Mochi, Kamati Mochi, Ranigar, Rohidas, Rohit, Samgar
5. Bhangi, Mehtar, Olgana, Rukhi, Malkana, Halalkhor, Latbegi, Balmiki, Korar, Zadmalli
6. Chalvadi, Channaya
7. Chenna Dasar, Holava Dasar
8. Dangashia
9. Dhor, Kakkayya, Kankayya
10. Garmatang
11. Garoda, Garo
12. Halleer
13. Halsar, Haslar, Hulasvar Halasvar
14. Holar, Vathar
15. Holaya, Holer
16. Lingader
17. Mahar, Taral, Dhegu Megu
18. Mahyavansi, Dhed, Dhedh, Vankar, Maru Vankar, Antyaj
19. Mang, Matang, Minimadig
20. Mang-Garudi
21. Meghval, Meghwal, Menghvar
22. Mukri
23. Nadia, Hadi
24. Pasi
25. Senva, Shenva, Chenva, Sedma, Rawat
26. Shemalia
27. Thori
28. Tirgar, Tirbanda
29. Turi
30. Turi Barot, Dedh Barot

SCHEDULED TRIBES

1. Barda
2. Bavacha, Bamcha
3. Bharwad (in the Nesses of the forests of Alech, Barada and Gir)
4. Bhil, Bhil Garasia, Dholi-Bhil, Dungri Bhil, Dungri Garasla, Mewasi Bhil, Rawal Bhil, Tadvi Bhil, Bhagalia, Bhilala, Pawra, Vasava, Vasave
5. Charan (in the Nesses of the forests of Alech, Barada and Gir)
6. Chaudhri (in Surat and Valsad districts)
7. Chodhara
8. Dhanka, Tadvi, Tetaria, Valvi
9. Dhodia
10. Dubla, Talavia, Halpati
11. Gamit, Gamta, Gavit, Mavchi Padvi
12. Gond, Rajgond
13. Kathodi, Katkari, Dhor Kathodi, Dhor Katkari, Son Kathodi, Son Katkari
14. Kokna, Kokni, Kukna
15. Koli (in Kutch district)

16. Koli Dhor, Tokre Koli, Kolcha, Kolgha
17. Kunbi (in the Dangs district)
18 Naikda, Nayaka, Cholivala Nayaka, Kapadia Nayaka, Mota Nayaka, Nana Nayaka
19. Podhar
20. Paradhi (in Kutch district)
21. Pardhi, Advichincher, Phanse Pardhi (excluding Amreli, Bhavnagar, Jamnagar, Junagadh, Kutch, Rajkot and Surendranagar districts)
22. Patelia
23. Pomla
24. Rabari (in the Nesses of the forests of Alech, Barada and Gir)
5. Rathawa
26. Siddi (in Amreli, Bhavnagar, Jamnagar, Junagadh, Rajkot and Surendranagar districts)
27. Vaghri (in Kutch district)
28. Varli
29. Vitola, Kotwalia, Barodia

HARYANA

[The Scheduled Castes and Scheduled Tribes Orders (Amendment) Act, 1976 (No. 108 of 1976, dated the 18th September, 1976)]

SCHEDULED CASTES

1. Ad Dharmi
2. Balmiki, Chura, Bhaing
3. Bangali
4. Barar, Burar, Berar
5. Batwal
6. Bauria, Bawaria
7. Bazigar
8. Bhanjra
9. Chamar, Jatia Chamar, Rehgar, Raigar, Ramdasi, Ravidasi
10. Chanal
11. Dagi
12. Darain
13. Deha, Dhaya, Dhea
14. Dhanak
15. Dhogri, Dhangri, Siggi
16. Dumna, Mahasha, Doom
17. Gagra
18. Gandhila, Gandil Gondola
19. Kabirpanthi, Julaha
20. Khatik
21. Kori, Koli
22. Maaij, Marecha
23. Mazhabi
24. Megh
25. Nat
26. Od
27. Pasi
28. Perna
29. Pherera
30. Sanhai
31. Sanhal
32. Sansi
33. Sansoi
34. Sapela
35. Sarera
36. Sikligar
37. Sirkiband

HIMACHAL PRADESH

[The Scheduled Castes and Scheduled Tribes Orders (Amendment) Act, 1976 (No. 108 of 1976, dated the 18th September, 1976)]

SCHEDULED CASTES

1. Ad Dhami
2. Badhi, Nagalu
3. Balmiki, Bhangi, Chuhra Chura, Chuhre
4. Bandhela
5. Bangali
6. Banjara
7. Bansi
8. Barad
9. Barar, Burar, Berar
10. Batwal
11. Bauria, Bawaria
12. Bazigar
13. Bhanjra, Bhanjre
14. Chamar, Jatia Chamar, Rehgar, Ramdasi, Ravidasi, Ramdasia, Mochi
15. Chanal
16. Chhimbe, Dhobi
17. Dagi
18. Darain
19. Darai, Daryai
20. Daule, Daole
21. Dhaki, Toori
22. Dhanak
23. Dhaogri, Dhuai
24. Dhogri. Dhangri, Siggi
25. Doom, Doomna, Dumna, Dumne, Mahasha
26. Gagra
27. Gandhila, Gandil, Gondola
28. Hali
29. Hesi
30. Jogi
31. Julaha, Julahe, Kabirpanthi, Keer
32. Kamoh, Dagoli
33. Karoack
34. Khatik
35. Kori, Koli
36. Lohar
37. Morija, Marecha
38. Mazhabi
39. Megh
40. Nat
41. Od
42. Pasi
43. Perna
44. Phrera, Pherera
45. Rehar, Rehara
46. Sanhai
47. Sanhal
48. Sansi, Bhedkut, Manesh
49. Sansoi
50. Sapela
51. Sarde, Sarera, Sarare, Saryare Sarehde
52. Sikligar
53. Sipi
54. Sirkiband
55. Teli
56. Thothiar, Thathera

SCHEDULED TRIBES

1. Bhot, Bodh
2. Gaddi [excluding the territories specified in sub-section (1) of section 5 of the Punjab Reorganisation Act, 1966 (31 of 1966), other than the Lahaul and Spiti district]
3. Gujjar [excluding the territories specified in sub-section (1) of section 5 of the Punjab Reorganisation Act, 1966 (31 of 1966)]
4. Jad, Lamba, Khampa
5. Kanaura, Kinnara
6. Lahaula
7. Pangwala
8. Swangla

JAMMU & KASHMIR

[The Constitution (Jammu & Kashmir) Scheduled Castes Order, 1956, C.O. 52]

SCHEDULED CASTES

1. Barwala
2. Basith
3. Batwal
4. Chamar or Ramdasia
5. Chura
6. Dhyar
7. Doom or Mahasha
8. Gardi
9. Jolaha
10. Megh or Kabirpanthi
11. Ratal
12. Saryara
13. Watal

KARNATAKA

[The Scheduled Castes and Scheduled Tribes Orders (Amendment) Act, 1976 (No. 108 of 1976, dated the 18th September, 1976)]

SCHEDULED CASTES

1. Adi Andhra
2. Adi Dravida
3. Adi Karnataka
4. Adiya (in Coorg district)
5. Ager
6. Ajila
7. Anamuk
8. Aray Mala
9. Arunthathiyar
10. Arwa Mala
11. Baira
12. Bakad
13. Bant (in Belgaum, Bijapur, Dharwar and North Kanara districts)
14. Bakuda
15. Balagai
16. Bandi
17. Banjara, Lambani
18. Bathada
19. Beda Jangam, Budga Jangam
20. Bellara
21. Bhangi, Mehtar, Olgana, Rukhi, Malkana, Halalkhor, Lalbegi, Balmiki, Korar, Zadmalli
22. Bhambi, Bhambhi, Asadaru, Asodi, Chamadia, Chamar, Chambhar, Chamgar, Haralayya, Harali, Khalpa, Machigar, Mochigar, Madar, Madig, Mochi, Muchi, Telegu Mochi, Kamati, Mochi, Ranigar, Rohidas, Rohit, Samgar
23. Bhovi
24. Bindla
25. Byagara
26. Chakkiliyan
27. Chalavadi, Chalvadi, Channayya
28. Chandala
29. Chenna Dasar, Holaya Dasar
30. Dakkal, Dokkalwar
31. Dakkaliga
32. Dhor, Kakkayya, Kankayya
33. Dom, Dombara, Paidi, Pano
34. Ellamalwar, Yellammalawandlu
35. Ganti Chores
36. Garoda, Garo
37. Godda

38. Gosangi
39. Halleer
40. Halsar, Haslar, Hulasvar, Halasvar
41. Handi Jogis
42. Hasla
43. Holar, Valhar
44. Holaya, Holer, Holeya
45. Holeya Dasari
46. Jaggali
47. Jambuvulu
48. Kadaiyan
49. Kalladi
50. Kepmaris
51. Kolupulvandlu
52. Koosa
53. Koracha
54. Rorama
55. Kotegar, Metri
56. Kudumban
57. Kuravan
58. Lingader
59. Machala
60. Madari
61. Madiga
62. Mahar, Taral, Dhegu Megu
63. Mahyavanshi, Dhed, Vankar, Maru Vankar
64. Maila
65. Mala
66. Mala Dasari
67. Mala Hannai
68. Mala Jangam
69. Mala Masti
70. Mala Sale, Netkani
71. Mala Sanyasi
72. Mang, Matang, Minimadig
73. Mang Garudi, Mang Garodi
74. Manne
75. Masthi
76. Mavilan
77. Meghval, Menghvar
78. Moger
79. Mukri
70. Mundala
81. MNadia, Hadi
82. Nalkadaya
83. Nalakeyava
84. Nayadi
85. Pale
86. Pallan
87. Pamboda
88. Panchama
89. Panniandi
90. Paraiyan, Paraya
91. Paravan
92. Raneyar
93. Samagara
94. Samban
95. Sapari
96. Sillekyathas
97. Sindhollu, Chindollu
98. Sudugadu Siddha
99. Thoti
100. Tirgar, Tirbanda
101. Valluvan

SCHEDULED TRIBES

1. Adiyan
2. Barda
3. Bavacha, Bamcha
4. Bhil, Bhil Garasia, Dholi Bhil, Dungri Bhil, Dungri Garasia, Mewasi Bhil, Rawal Bhil, Tadvi Bhil, Bhagalia, Bhilala, Pawra, Vasava, Vasave
5. Chenchu, Chenchwar
6. Chodhara
7. Dubla, Talavia, Halpati
8. Gamit, Gamta, Gavit, Mavchi, Padvi, Valvi
9. Gond, Naikpod, Rajgond
10. Gowdalu
11. Hakkipikki
12. Hasalaru
13. Irular
14. Iruliga
15. Jenu Kuruba
16. Kadu kuruba
17. Kammaga (in Soutti Kanara

district and Kollegal taluk of Mysore district)
18. Kaniyan, Kanyan (in Kollegal taluk of Mysore district)
19. Kathodi, Katkari, Dhor, Kathodi, Dhor Katkari, Son Kathodi, Son Katkari
20. Kattunayakan
21. Kokna, Kokni, Kukna
22. Koli, Dhor, Tokre Koli, Kolcha, Kolgha
23. Konda Kapus
24. Koraga
25. Kota
26. Koya, Bhine Koya, Rajkoya
27. Kudiya, Melakudi
28. Kuruba (in Coorg district)
29. Kurumans
30. Maha Malasar
31. Malaikudi
32. Malasar
33. Malayekandi
34. Maleru
35. Maratha (in Coorg district)
36. Marati (in South Kanara district)
37. Meda
38. Naikda, Nayaka, Cholivala Nayaka, Kapadia Nayaka, Mota, Nayaka, Nana Nayaka
39. Palliyam
40. Paniyan
41. Pardhi, Advichincher, Phanse Pardhi
42. Patelia
43. Rathawa
44. Sholaga
45. Soligaru
46. Toda
47. Varli
48. Vitolia, Kotwalia, Barodia
49. Yerava

KERALA

(The Scheduled Castes and Scheduled Tribes Orders (Amendment) Act, 1976 No. 108 of 1976, dated the 18th September 1976)

SCHEDULED CASTES

1. Adi Andhra
2. Adi Dravida
3. Adi Karnataka
4. Ajila
5. Arunthathiyar
6. Ayyanavar
7. Baira
8. Bakuda
9. Bandi
10. Bathada
11. Bellara
12. Bharatar
13. Boyan (excluding the areas comprising the Malabar district as specified by sub-section (2) of section 5 of the States Reorganisation Act, 1956 (37 of 1956))
14. Chakkiliyan
15. Chamar, Muchi
16. Chandala
17. Cheruman
18. Domban
19. Gavara
20. Godagali
21. Godda
22. Gosangi
23. Hesla
24. Holeya
25. Kadaiyan
26. Kakkalan
27. Kalladi
28. Kanakkan, Padanna
29. Karimpalan
30. Kavara
31. Koosa

32. Kootan, Koodan
33. Kudumban
34. Kuravan, Sidhanar
35. Maila
36. Malayan [in the areas comprising the Malabar district as specified by sub-section (2) of section of the States Reorganisation Act, 1956 (37 of 1956)]
37. Mannan
38. Mavilan
39. Moger
40. Mundala
41. Nalakeyava
42. Nalkadaya
43. Nayadi
44. Padannan
45. Pallan
47. Palluvan
46. Pambada
48. Panan
49. Panchama
50. Paraiyan, Parayan, Sambavar
51. Paravan
52. Pathiyan
53. Perumannan
54. Pulayan, Cheramar
55. Pulaya Vettuvan
56. Puthirai Vannan
57. Raneyar
58. Samagara
59. Samban
60. Semman
61. Thandan
62. Thoti
63. Vallon
64. Valluvan
65. Vannan
66. Velan
67. Vetan
68. Vettuvan

SCHEDULED TRIBES

1. Adiyan
2. Arandan
3. Eravallan
4. Hill Pulaya
5. Irular, Irulan
6. Kadar
7. Kammara [in the areas comprising the Malabar district as specified by sub-section 2 of section 5 of the States Reorganisation Act, 1956 (37) of 1956)]
8. Kanikaran, Kanikkar
9. Kattunayakan
10. Kochu Velan
11. Konda Kapus
12. Kondareddis
13. Koraga
14. Kota
15. Kudiya, Melakudi
16. Kurichchan
17. Kurumans
18. Kurumbas
19. Maha Malasar
20. Malai Arayan
21. Malai Pandaram
22. Malai Vedan
23. Malakkuravan
24. Malasar
25. Malayan [excluding the areas comprising the Malabar district as specified by subsection (2)of section 5 of the States Reorganisation Act, 1956 (37 of 1956)]
26. Malayarayar
27. Mannan
28. Marati (in Hosdurg and Kasaragod taluks of Cannanore district
29. Muthuvan, Mudugar, Muduvan
30. Paiieyan
31. Paeliyan
32. Palliyar
33. Paniyan
34. Ulladan
35. Uraly

MADHYA PRADESH

[The Scheduled Castes and Scheduled Tribes Orders (Amendment) Act, 1976 (No. 108 of 1976, dated the 18th September, 1976)]

SCHEDULED CASTES

1. Audhelia
2. Bagri, Bagdi
3. Bahna, Bahana
4. Balahi, Balai
5. Banchada
6. Barahar, Basod
7. Bargunda
8. Basor, Burud, Bansor, Bansodi, Bansphor, Basar
9. Bedia
10. Beldar, Sunkar
11. Bhangi, Mehtar, Balmik, Lalbegi, Dharkar
12. Bhanumati
13. Chadar
14. Chamar, Chamari, Bairwa, Bhambi, Jatav, Mochi, Regar, Nona, Rohidas, Ramnami, Satnami, Surjyabanshi, Surjyaramnami, Ahirwnr, Chamar Mangan, Raidas
15. Chidar
16. Chikwa, Chikvi
17. Chitar
18. Dahait, Dahayat, Dahat
19. Dewar
20. Dhanuk
21. Dhed, Dher
22. Dhobi(in Bhopal, Raisen and Sehore districts)
23. Dohor
24. Dom, Dumar, Dome, Domar, Doris
25. Ganda, Gandi
26. Ghasi, Ghasia
27. Holiya
28. Kanjar
29. Katia, Patharia
30. Khatik
31. Koli, Kori
32. Kotwal (in Bhind, Dhar, Dewas, Guna, Gwalior, Indore Jhabua, Khargone, Mandsaur, Morena, Rajgarh, Ratlam Shajapur, Shivpuri, Ujjain, and Vidisha districts)
33. Khangar, Kanera, Mirdha
34. Kuchbandhia
35. Kumhar (in Chhatarpur, Datia, Panna, Rewa, Satna, Shahdol, Sidhi and Tikamgarh districts)
36. Mahar, Mehra, Mehar
37. Mang, Mang Garodi, Mang Garudi, Dankhni Mang, Mang Mahasi, Madari, Garudi, Radhe Mang
38. Meghwal
39. Moghia
40. Muskhan
41. Nat, Kalbelia, Sapera Navdigar, Kubutar
42. Pardhi (in Bhind, Dhar, Dewas, Guna, Gwalior,Indore Jhabua, Khargone, Mandsaur, Morena, Rajgarh, Ratlam, Shajapur, Shivpuri, Ujjain and Vidisha districts)
43. Pasi
44. Rujjhar
45. Sansi, Sansia
46. Silawat
47. Zamral

SCHEDULED TRIBES

1. Agariya
2. Andh
3. Baiga
4. Bhaina
5. Bharia Bhumia. Bhuinhar, Bhumia, Bhumiya, Bharia, Paliha, Pando
6. Bhattra
7. Bhil, Bhilala, Barela, Patelia
8. Bhil Mina
9. Bhunjia
10. Biar, Biyar
11. Binjhwar
12. Birhul, Birhor
13. Damor, Damaria
14. Dhanwar
15 Gadaba, Gadba
16. Gond, Arakh, Arrakh, Agaria Asur, Badi Maria, Bada Maria, Bhatola, Bhimma, Bhuta, Koilabhuta, Koliabhuti, Bhar, Bisonhorn Maria, Chota Maria, Dandami Maria, Dhuru, Dhurwa, Dhoba, Dhulia, Doria, Gaiki, Gatta, Gatti, Gaita, Gond Gowari, Hill Maria, Kandra, Knalaga, Khatola, Koitar, Koya, Khirwar, Khirwara, Kucha Maria, Kuchaki Maria Madia, Maria, Mana, Mannewar, Moghya, Mogia, Monghya, Mudia. Muria, Nagarchi Nagwanshi, Ojha, Raj, Sonjhari Jhareka, Thatia, Thotya, Wade Maria, Vade Maria, Daroi
17. Haiba, Haibi
18. Kamar
19. Karku
20. Kawar, Kanwar, Kaur, Cherwa, Rathia, Tanwar, Chattri
21. Keer (in Bhopal, Ralsen and Sehore districts)
22. Khairwar, Kondar
23. Kharia
24. Kondh, Khond, Kandh
25. Kol
26. Kolam
27. Korku, Bopchi. Mouasi, Nihal, Nahul, Bondhi, Bondeya
28. Korwa, Kodaku
29. Majhi
30. Majhwar
31. Mawasi
32. Mina (in Sironj sub-division of Vidisha district)
33. Munda
34. Nagesia, Nagasia
35. Oraon, Dhanka, Dhangad
36. Panika (in Chhatarpur, Datia Panna, Rewa, Satna, Shahdol, Sidhi and Tikamgarh districts)
37. Pao
38. Pardhan, Pathari, Saroti
39. Pardhi (in Bhopal, Raisen and Sehore districts)
40. Parhi, Bahelia, Bahellia, Chita Pardhi, Langoli Pardhi, Phanse Pardhi, Shikari, Takankar, Takia [in (1) Bastar Chhindwara, Mandla, Raigarh Seoni and Surguja districts, (2) Baihar tahsil of Balaghat district, (3) Betul and Bhainsdehi tahsils of Betul district, (4) Bilaspur and Katghora tahsils of Bilaspur district, (5) Durg and Balod tahsils of Durg district, (6) Chowki, Manpur and Mohala Revenue Inspectors' Circles of Rajnandgaon district, (7) Murwara, Patan and Sihora tahsils of Jabalpur district, (8) Hoshangabad and Sohagpur tahsils of Hoshangabad district and Narsimhapur district, (9) Harsud tahsil of Khandwa

district, (10) Bindra-Nawagarh, Dhamtari and Mahasamund tahsils of Rajpur district]
41. Parja
42. Sahariya, Saharia, Seharia, Sosia, Sor
43. Saonta, Saunta
44. Saur
45. Sawar, Sawara
46. Sonr

MAHARASHTRA

[The Scheduled Castes and Scheduled Tribes Orders (Amendment) Act, 1976 (No. 108 of 1976, dated the 18th September, 1976)]

SCHEDULED CASTES

1. Ager
2. Anamuk
3. Aray Mala
4. Arwa Mala
5. Bahna, Bahana
6. Bakad, Bant
7. Balahi, Balai
8. Basor, Burud, Bansor, Bansodi
9. Beda Jangam, Budga Jangam
10. Bedar
11. Bhambi, Bhambhi, Asadaru, Asodi, Chamadia, Chamar, Chamari, Chambhar, Chamgar, Haralayya, Harali, Khalpa, Machigar, Mochigar, Madar, Madig, Mochi, Telcgu Mochi, Kamati Mochi, Raniga, Rohidas, Nona, Ramnami, Rohit, Samgar, Samagara, Satnami, Surjyabanshi, Surjyaramnami
12. Bhangi, Mehtar, Olgana, Rukhi, Malkana, Halalkhor, Lalbegl, Balmiki, Korar, Zadmalli
13. Bindla
14. Byagara
15. Chalvadi, Channayya
16. Chenna Dasar, Holaya Dasar, Holeya Dasari
17. Dakkal, Dokkalwar
18. Dhor, Kakkayya, Kankayya, Dohor
19. Dom, Dumar
20. Ellamalvar, Yellammalawandlu
21. Ganda, Gandi
22. Garoda, Garo
23. Ghasi, Ghasia
24. Halleer
25. Halsar, Haslar, Hulasvar, Halasvar
26. Holar, Valhar
27. Holaya, Holer, Holeya, Holiya
28. Kai7adi (in Akola Amravati, Bhandara Buldana, Nagpur, Wardha and Yavatmal districts and Chandrapur districts, other than Rajura tahsil)
29. Katia, Patharia
30. Khangar, Kanera, Mirdha
31. Katik, Chikwa, Chikvi
32. Kolupulvandlu
33, Kori
34. Lingader
35. Madgi
36. Madiga
37. Mahar, Mehra, Taral, Dhegu Megu
38, Mahyavanshi, Dhed, Vankar, Maru Vankar

39. Mala
40. Mala Dasari
41. Mala Hannai
42. Mala Jangam
43. Mala Masti
44. Mala Sale, Netkani
45. Mala Sanyasi
46. Mang, Matang, Minimadig, Dankhni Mang, Mang, Mahashi, Madari, Garudi, Radhe Mang
47. Mang Garodi, Mang Garudi
48. Manne
49. Mashti
50. Meghval, Menghvar
51. Mitha Ayyalvar
52. Mukri
53. Nadia, Hadi
54. Pasi
55. Sansi
56. Shenva, Cheva, Sedma, Ravat
57. Sindhollu, Chindollu
58. Tirgar, Tirbanda
59. Turi

SCHEDULED TRIBES

1. Andh
2. Baiga
3. Barda
4. Bavacha, Bamcha
5. Bhaina
6. Bharia Bhumia, Bhuinhar Bhumia, Pando
7. Bhattra
8. Bhil, Bhil Garasia, Dholi Bhil, Dungri Bhil, Dungri Garasia, Mewasi Bhil, Rawal Bhil, Tadvi Bhil, Bhagalia, Bhilala, Pawra, Vasava, Vassave
9. Bhunjia
10. Binjhwar
11. Birhul, Birhor
12. Chodhara (excluding Akola, Amravati, Bhandara, Buldana, Chandrapur, Nagpur, Wardha, Yavatmal, Aurangabad, Bhir, Nanded, Osmanabad and Parbhani districts)
13. Dhanka, Tadvi, Tetaria, Valvi
14. Dhanwar
15. Dhodia
16. Dubla, Talavia, Halpati
17. Gamit, Gamta Gavit, Mavchi, Padvi
18. Gond, Rajgond, Arakh, Arrakh, Agaria, Asur, Badi Maria, Bada Maria, Bhatola, Bhimma Bhuta, Koilabhuta, Koilabhuti, Bhar, Bisonhorn, Maria, Chota Maria, Dandami Maria, Dhuru, Dhurwa, Dhoba Dhulia, Doria, Gaiki, Gatta, Gatti, Gaita, Gond Gowari, Hill Maria, Kandra, Kalanga Khatola, Koitar, Koya, Khirwar, Khirwara, Kucha Maria, Kuchaki Maria, Madia, Maria, Mana, Mannewar, Modghya, Mogia, Monghya, Mudia, Muria, Nagarchi, Naikpod, Nagwanshi, Ojha, Raj Sonjhari Jhareka, Thatia, Thotya, Wade Maria, Vade Maria.
19. Halba, Halbi
20. Kamar
21. Kathodi, Katkari, Dhor Kathodi, Dhor Katkari, Son Kathodi, Son Katkari
22. Kawar, Kanwar, Kaur, Cherwa, Rathia, Tanwar, Chattri
23. Khairwar
24. Kharia
25. Kokna, Kokni, Kukna
26. Kol
27. Kolam, Mannervarlu
28. Koli, Dhor, Tokre Koli,

Kolcha, Kolgha
29. Koli Mahadev, Dongar Koli
30. Koli Malhar
31. Kondh, Khond, Kandh
32. Korku, Bopchi, Mouasi, Nihal, Nahul, Bondhi, Bondeya
33. Koya, Bhine Koya, Rajkoya
34. Nagesia, Nagasia
35. Naikda, Nayaka, Cholivala Nayaka, Kapadia Nayaka, Mota Nayaka, Nana Nayaka
36. Oraon, Dhangad
37. Pardhan, Pathari, Saroti
38. Pardhi, Advichincher, Phanse Pardhi, Phanse Pardhi, Langoli Pardhi, Bahelia, Bahellia Chita Pardhi, Shikari, Takankar, Takia
39. Parja
40. Patelia
41. Pomla
42. Rathawa
43. Sawar, Sawara
44. Thakur, Thakar, Ka Thakur, Ka Thakar, Ma Thakur, Ma Thakar
45. Thoti (in Auragabad, Bhir, Nanded, Osmanabad and Parbhani districts and Rajura tahsil of Chandrapur district)
46. Varli
47. Vitolia, Kotwalia, Barodia

MANIPUR

[The Scheduled Castes and Scheduled Tribes Orders (Amendment) Act, 1976 (No. 108 of 1976, dated the 18th September, 1976)]

SCHEDULED CASTES

1. Dhupi, Dhobi
2. Lois
3. Muchi, Ravidas
4. Namasudra
5. Patni
6. Sutradhar
7. Yaithibi

SCHEDULED TRIBES

1. Aimol
2. Anal
3. Angami
4. Chiru
5. Chothe
6. Gangte
7. Hmar
8. Kabui
9. Kacha Naga
10. Koirao
11. Koireng
12. Kom
13. Lamgang
14. Mao
15. Maram
16. Maring
17. Any Mizo (Lushai) tribes
18. Monsang
19. Moyon
20. Paite
21. Purum
22. Ralte
23. Sema
24. Simte
25. Sahte
26. Tangkhul
27. Thadou
28. Vaiphui
29. Zou

MEGHALAYA

[The Scheduled Castes and Scheduled Tribes Orders (Amendment) Act, 1976 (No. 108 of 1976, dated the 18th September, 1976)]

SCHEDULED CASTES

1. Bansphor
2. Bhuinmali, Mali
3. Brittial Bania, Bania
4. Dhupi, Dhobi
5. Dugla, Dholi
6. Hira
7. Jalkeot
8. Jhalo, Malo, Jhalo-Malo
9. Kaibartta, Jaliya
10. Lalbegi
11. Mahara
12. Mehtar, Bhangi
13. Muchi, Rishi
14. Namasudra
15. Patni
16. Sutradhar

SCHEDULED TRIBES

1. Chakma
2. Dimasa, Kachari
3. Garo
4. Hajong
5. Hmar
6. Khasi, Jaintia, Synteng, Pnar, War, Bhoi, Lyngngam
7. Any Kuki Tribes, including :
   (i) Biate, Biete
   (ii) Changsan
   (iii) Chongloi
   (iv) Doungel
   (v) Gamalhou
   (vi) Gangte
   (vii) Guite
   (viii) Hanneng
   (ix) Haokip, Haupit
   (x) Haolai
   (xi) Hengna
   (xii) Hongsungh
   (xiii) Hrangkhwal, Rangkhol
   (xiv) Jongbe
   (xv) Khawchung
   (xvi) Khawathlang, Khothalong
   (xvii) Khelma
   (xviii) Kholhou
   (xix) Kipgan
   (xx) Kuki
   (xxi) Lengthang
   (xxii) Lhangum
   (xxiii) Lhoujem
   (xxiv) Lhouvun
   (xxv) Lupheng
   (xxvi) Mangjel
   (xxvii) Misao
   (xxviii) Riang
   (xxix) Sairhem
   (xxx) Selnam
   (xxxi) Singson
   (xxxii) Sitlhou
   (xxxiii) Sukte
   (xxxiv) Thado
   (xxxv) Thangngen
   (xxxvi) Uibuh
   (xxxvii) Vaiphei
8. Lakher
9. Man (Tai speaking)
10. Any Mizo (Lushai) tribes
11. Mikir
12. Any Naga tribes
13. Pawi
14. Synteng

NAGALAND

[The Constitution (Nagaland) Scheduled Tribes Order, 1970. C.O. 88]

SCHEDULED TRIBES

1. Garo
2. Kachari
2. Kuki
4. Mikir
5. Naga

ORISSA

[The Scheduled Castes and Scheduled Tribes Orders (Amendment) Act, 1976 (No. 108 of 1976 dated the 18th september, 1976)]

SCHEDULED CASTES

1. Adi Andhra
2. Amant, Amat
3. Audhelia
4. Badaik
5. Bagheti, Baghuti
6. Bajikar
7. Bari
8. Bariki
9. Basor, Burud
10. Bauri
11. Bauti
12. Bavuri
13. Bedi, Bejia
14. Beldar
15. Bhata
16. Bhoi
17. Chachati
18. Chakali
19. Chamar, Mochi, Muchi, Satnami
20. Chandala
21. Chandhai Maru
22. Cherua, Chhelia
23. Dandasi
24. Dewar
25. Dhanwar
26. Dhoba, Dhobi
27. Dom, Dombo, Duria Dom
18. Dosadha
29. Ganda
30. Ghantarghada, Ghantra
31. Ghasi, Ghasia
32. Ghogia
33. Ghusuria
34. Godagali
35. Godari
36. Godra
37. Gokha
38. Gorait, Korait
39. Haddi, Hadi, Hari
40. Irika
41. Jaggali
42. Kandra, Kandara
43. Karua
44. Katia
45. Kela
46. Khadala
47. Kodalo, Khodalo
48. Kori
49. Kummari
50. Kurunga
51. Laban
52. Laheri
53. Madari
54. Madiga
55. Mahuria

56. Mala, Jhala, Malo, Zala
57. Mang
58. Mangan
59. Mehra Mahar
60. Mehtar, Bhangi
61. Mewar
62. Mundapotta
63. Musahar
64. Nagarchi
65. Namasudra
66. Paidi
67. Painda
68. Pamidi
69. Pan, Pano
70. Panchama
71. Pantanti
72. Panika
73. Panka
74. Pap
75. Pasi
76. Patial Patikar, Patratanti, Patua
77. Rajna
78. Relli
79. Sabakhia
80. Samasi
81. Sanei
82. Sapari
83. Sauntia, Santia
84. Sidhria
85. Sinduria
86. Siyal
87. Tamadia
88. Tamudia
89. Tanla
90. Tiar, Tior
91. Turi
92. Ujia
93. Valamiki, Valmiki

SCHEDULED TRIBES

1. Bagata
2. Baiga
3. Banjara, Banjari
4. Bathudi
5. Bhottada, Dhotada
6. Bhuiya, Bhuyan
7. Bhumia
8. Bhumij
9. Bhunjia
10. Binjhal
11. Binjhia, Binjhoa
12. Birhor
13. Bondo Poraja
14. Chenchu
15. Dal
16. Desua Bhumij
17. Dharua
18. Didayi
19. Gadaba
20. Gandia
21. Ghara
22. Gond, Gondo
23. Ho
24. Holva
25. Jatapu
26. Juang
27. Kandha Gauda
28. Kawar
29. Kharia. Kharian
30. Kharwar
31. Khond, Kond, Kandha, Nanguli Kandha, Sitha Kandha
32. Kisan
33. Kol
34. Kolah Loharas, Kol Loharas
35. Kolha
36. Koli, Malhar
37. Kondadora
38. Kora
39. Korua
40. Kotia
41. Koya
42. Kulis
43. Lodha
44. Madia
45. Mahali

46. Manakidi
47. Mankirdia
48. Matya
49. Mirdhas
50. Munda, Munda Lohara, Munda Mahalis
51. Mundari
52. Omanatya
53. Oraon
54. Parenga
55. Paroja
56. Pentia
57. Rajuar
58. Santal
59. Saora, Savar, Saura, Sahara
60. Shabar, Lodha
61. Sounti
62. Tharua

PUNJAB

[The Scheduled Castes and Scheduled Tribes Orders (Amendment) Act, 1976 (No. 108 of 1976, dated the 18th September, 1976)]

SCHEDULED CASTES

1. Ad Dharmi
2. Balmiki, Chuhra, Bhangi
3. Bangali
4. Barar, Burar, Berar
5. Batwal
6. Bauria, Bawaria
7. Bazigar
8. Bhanjra
9. Chamar, Jatia Chamar, Rehgar, Raigar, Ramdasi, Ravidasi
10. Chanal
11. Dagi
12. Darain
13. Deha, Dhaya, Dhea
14. Dhanak
15. Dhogri Dhangri, Siggi
16. Dumna, Mahasha, Doom
17. Gagra
18. Gandhila, Gandil Gondola
19. Kabirpanthi Julaha
20. Khatik
21. Kori, Koli
22. Marija, Marecha
23. Mazhabi
24. Megh
25. Nat
26. Od
27. Pasi
28. Perma
29. Pherera
30. Sanhai
31. Sanhal
32. Sansi, Bhedkut, Manesh
33. Sansoi
34. Sapela
35. Sarera
36. Sikligar
37. Sirkiband

RAJASTHAN

[The Scbeduled Castes and Scheduled Tribes Orders (Amendment) Act, 1976 (No. 108 of 1976, dated the 18th September, 1976)]

SCHEDULED CASTES

1. Adi Dharmi
2. Aheri
3. Badi
4. Bagri, Bagdi
5. Bainwa, Berwa
6. Bajgar
7. Balai
8. Bansphor, Bansphod
9. Baori
10. Bargi, Vargi, Birgi
11. Bawaria
12. Bedia, Beria
13. Bhand
14. Bhangi, Chura, Mehtar, Olgana, Rukhi, Malkana, Halalkhor, Lalbegi. Balmiki, Valmiki, Korer, Zedmali
15. Bidakia
16. Bola
17. Chamar, Bhambhi, Bhambi, Jatia, Jatav, Jatava, Mochi Raidas, Rohidas, Regar, Raigar, Ramdasia, Asadaru, Asodi, Chamadia, Chambhar Chamgar, Haralayya, Hara Khalpa, Machigar, Mochigar, Madar, Madig, Telegu Mochi, Kamati, Mochi Ranigar, Rohit, Samgar
18. Chandal
19. Dabgar
20. Dhanak, Dhanuk
21. Dhankia
22. Dhobi
23. Dholi
24. Dome, Dom
25. Gandia
26. Garancha, Gancha
27. Garo, Garura, Gurda, Garoda
28. Gavaria
29. Godhi
30. Jingar
31. Kalbalia, Sapera
32. Kamad, Kamedia
33. Kanjar, Kunjar,
34. Kapadli Sansi
35. Khangar
36. Khatik
37. Koli, Kori
38. Koach Band, Kuchband
39. Koria
40. Madari, Bazigar
41. Mahar, Taral Dhegumegu
42. Mahysvashi, Dhed, Dheda Vankar, Maru, Vankar
43. Majhabi
44. Mang, Matang, Minimedig
45. Mang Garodi, Mang Garudi
46. Megh, Meghval, Meghwal, Manghvar
47. Mahar
48. Nat Nut,
49. Pasi
50. Rawal
51. Salvi
52. Sansi
53. Santia Satia
54. Sarbhangi
55. Sargara
56. Singiwala
57. Thori, Nayak
58. Tirgar, Tirbanda
59. Turi

SCHEDULED TRIBES

1. Bhil, Bhil Garasia, Dholi Bhil, Dungri Bhil, Dung Garasia, Mawasi Bhil, Rawal, Bhil, Tadvi Bhil, Bhagalia Bhilala, Pawra, Vasava, Vasave
2. Bhil Mina
3. Damor, Damaria
4. Dhanka, Tadvi, Tetaria, Valvi
5. Garasia (excluding Rajput Garasia)
6. Kathodi, Katkari, Dhor Kathodi, Dhor Katkari, Son Kathodi, Son Katkari
7. Kokna, Kokni, Kukna
8. Koli Dhor, Tokre Koli, Kolcha, Kolgha
9. Mina
10. Naikda, Nayaka, Cholivala Nayaka, Kapadia Nayaka, Mota Nayaka, Nana Nayaka
11. Patelia
12. Seharia, Sehria, Sahariya

SIKKIM

[The Constitution (Sikkim) Scheduled Castes Order, 1978, C.O. 110]

SCHEDULED CASTES

1. Damai (Nepali)
2. Kami (Nepali), Lohar, (Nepali)
3. Majhi (Nepali)
4. Sarki (Nepali)

[The Constitution (Sikkim) Scheduled Tribes Order, 1978]

SCHEDULED TRIBES

1. Bhutia (including Chumbipa, Dopthapa, Dukpa, Kagatey, Sherpa, Tibetan, Tromopa, Yolmo)
2. Lepcha

TAMIL NADU

[The Scheduled Castes and Scheduled Tribes Orders (Amendment) Act, 1976 (No. 108 of 1976, dated the 18th September, 1976)]

SCHEDULED CASTES

1. Adi Andhra
2. Adi Dravida
3. Adi Karnataka
4. Ajila
5. Arunthathiyar
6. Ayyanavar (in Kanyakumari district and Shenkottah taluk of Tirunelveli district)
7. Baira
8. Bakuda
9. Bandi
10. Bellara
11. Bharatar (in Kanyakumari district and Shenkottah taluk of Tirunelveli district)
12. Chakkiliyan

3. Chalavadi
14. Chamar, Muchi
15. Chandala
16. Cheruman
17. Devendrakulathan
18. Dom, Dombara, Paidi, Pano
19. Domban
20. Godagali
21. *Godda*
22. Gosangi
23. Holeya
24. Jaggali
25. Jambuvulu
26. Kadaiyan
27. Kakkalan (in Kanyakumari district and Shenkottah taluk of Tirunelveli district)
28. Kalladi
29. Kanakkan, Padanna (in the Nilgiris district)
30. Karimpalan
31. Kavara (in Kanyakumari district and Shenkottah taluk of Tirunelveli district)
32. Koliyan
33. Koosa
34. Kootan, Koodan (in Kanyakumari district and Shenkottah taluk of Tirunelveli district)
35. Kudumban
36. Kuravan, Sidhanar
37. Madari
38. Madiga
39. Maila
40. Mala
41. Mannan (in Kanyakumari district and Shenkottah taluk of Tirunelveli district)
42. Mavilan
43. Moger
44. Mundala
45. Nalakeyava
46. Nayadi
47. Padannan (in Kanyakumari district and Shenkottah taluk of Tirunelveli district)
48. Pagadai
49. Pallan
50. Palluvan
51. Pambada
52. Panan (in Kanyakumari district and Shenkottah tulak *of Tirunelveli district)*
53. Panchama
54. Pannadi
55. Panniandi
56. Paralyan, Parayan, Sambavar
57. Paravan (in Kanyakumari district and Shenkottah taluk of Tirunelveli district)
58. Pathiyan (in Kanyakumari district and Shenkottah taluk of Tirunelveli district)
59. Pulayan, Cheramar
60. Puthirai Vannan
61. Raneyar
62. Samagara
63. Samban
64. Sapari
65. Semman
66. Thandan (in Kanyakumari district and Shenkottah taluk of Tirunelveli district)
67. Thoti
68. Tiruvalluvar
69. Vallon
70. Valluvan
71. Vannan (in Kanyakumari district and Shenkottah taluk of Tirunelveli district)
72. Vathiriyan
73. Velan
74. Vetan (in Kanyakumari district and Shenkottah taluk of Tirunelveli district)
75. Vattiyan
76. Vettuvan (in Kanyakumari district and Shenkottah taluk of Tirunelveli district)

SCHEDULED TRIBES

1. Adiyan
2. Aranadan
3. Eravallan
4. Irular
5. Kadar
6. Kammara (excluding Kanyakumari district and Shenkottah taluk of Tirunelveli district)
7. Kanikaran, Kanikkar (in Kanyakumari district and Shenkottah taluk of Tirunelveli district)
8. Kaniyan, Kanyan
9. Kattunayakan
10. Kochu Velan
11. Konda Kapus
12. Kondareddis
13. Koraga
14. Kota (excluding Kanyakumari district and Shenkottah taluk of Tirunelveli district)
15. Kudiya, Melakudi
16. Kurichchan
17. Kurumbas (in the Nilgiris district)
18. Kurumans
19. Maha Malasar
20. Malai Arayan
21. Malai Pandaram
22. Malai Vedan
23. Malakkuravan
24. Malasar
25. Malayali (in Dharmapuri, North Arcot, Pudukottai, Salem, South Arcot and Tiruchirapalli districts)
26. Malayekandi
27. Mannan
28. Muduger, Muduvan
29. Muthuvan
30. Palleyan
31. Palliyan
32. Palliyar
33. Paniyan
34. Sholaga
35. Toda (including Kanyakumari district and Shenkottah taluk of Tirunelveli district)
36. Uraly

TRIPURA

[The Scheduled Castes and Scheduled Tribes Orders (Amendment) Act, 1976 (No. 108 of 1976, dated the 18th September, 1976)]

SCHEDULED CASTES

1. Bagdi
2. Bhuimall
3. Bhunar
4. Chamar, Muchi
5. Dandasi
6. Dhenuar
7. Dhoba
8. Dum
9. Ghasi
10. Gour
11. Gur
12. Jalia Kaibarta
13. Kahar
14. Kalindi
15. Kan
16. Kanda
17. Kanugh
18. Keot
19. Khadit
20. Kharia
21. Koch
22. Koir

23. Kol
24. Kora
25. Kotal
26. Mahisyadas
27. Mali
28. Mehtor
29. Musahar
30. Namasudra
31. Patni
32. Sabar

SCHEDULED TRIBES

1. Bhil
2. Bhutia
3. Chaimal
4. Chakma
5. Garoo
6. Halam
7. Jamatia
8. Khasia
9. Kuki, including the following sub-tribes :
   (i) Balte
   (ii) Belalhut
   (iii) Chhalya
   (iv) Fun
   (v) Hajango
   (vi) Jangtei
   (vii) Khareng
   (viii) Khephong
   (ix) Kuntel
   (x) Laifang
   (xi) Lentei
   (xii) Mizel
   (xiii) Namte
   (xiv) Paitu, Paite
   (xv) Rangchan
   (xvi) Rangkhole
   (xvii) Thangluya
10. Lepcha
11. Lushai
12. Mag
13. Munda, Kaur
14. Noatia
15. Orang
16. Riang
17. Santal
18. Tripura, Tripuri, Tippera
19. Uchai

UTTAR PRADESH

[The Scheduled Castes and Scheduled Tibes Orders (Amendment) Act, 1976 (No. 108 of 1976, dated the 18th September, 1976)]

SCHEDULED CASTES

1. Agariya
2. Badhik
3. Badi
4. Baheliya
5. Baiga
6. Balswar
7. Bajaniya
8. Bajgi
9. Balahar
10, Balai
11. Balmiki
12. Bangali
13. Banmanus
14. Bansphor
15. Barwar
16. Basor
17. Bawariya
18. Beldar
19. Beriya
20. Bhantu
21. Bhuiya
22. Bhuyiar

23. Boria
24. Chamar, Dhusia, Jhusia, Jatava
25. Chero
26. Dabgar
27. Dhangar
28. Dhanuk
29. Dharkar
30. Dhobi
31. Dom
32. Domar
33. Dusadh
34. Gharami
35. Ghasiya
36. Gond
37. Gual
38. Habura
39. Hari
40. Hela
41. Kalabaz
42. Kanjar
43. Kapariya
44. Karwal
45. Khairaha
46. Kharwar (excluding Benbansi)
47. Khatik
48. Khorot
49. Kol
50. Kori
51. Korwa
52. Lalbegi
53. Majhwar
54. Mazhabi
55. Musahar
56. Nat
57. Pankha
58. Parahiya
59. Pasi, Tarmali
60. Patari
61. Rawat
62. Saharya
63. Sanaurhiya
64. Sansiya
65. Shilpkar
66. Turaiha

[The Constitution (Scheduled Tribes) (Uttar Pradesh) Order, 1967, C.O. 78]

SCHEDULED TRIBES

1. Bhotia
2. Buksa
3. Jaunsari
4. Raji
5. Tharu

WEST BENGAL

[The Scheduled Castes and Scheduled Tribes Orders (Amendment) Act, 1976 (No. 108 of 1976, dated the 18th September, 1976)]

SCHEDULED CASTES

1. Bagdi, Duley
2. Bahelia
3. Baiti
4. Bantar
5. Bauri
6. Beldar
7. Bhogta
8. Bhuimali
9. Bhuiya
10. Bind
11. Chamar, Charmakar, Mochi, Muchi, Rabidas, Ruidas, Rishi
12. Chaupal
13. Dabgar
14. Damai (Nepali)
15. Dhoba, Dhobi

16. Doal
17. Dom, Dhangad
18. Dosadh, Dusadh, Dhari, Dharhi
19. Ghasi
20. Gonrhi
21. Halalkhor
22. Hari, Mehtar, Mehtor, Bhangi
23. Jalia Kaibartta
24. Jhalo Malo, Malo
25. Kadar
26. Kami (Nepali)
27. Kandra
28. Kanjar
29. Kaora
30. Karenga, Koranga
31. Kaur
32. Keot, Keyot
33. Khaira
34. Khatik
35. Koch
36. Konai
37. Konwar
38. Kotal
39. Kurariar
40. Lalbegi
41. Lohar
42. Mahar
43. Mal
44. Mallah
45. Musahar
46. Namasudra
47. Nat
48. Nuniya
49. Paliya
50. Pan, Sawasi
51. Pasi
52. Patni
53. Pod, Poundra
54. Rajbanshi
55. Rajwar
56. Sarki (Nepali)
57. Sunri (excluding Saha)
58. Tiyar
59. Turi

SCHEDULED TRIBES

1. Asur
2. Baiga
3. Bedia, Bediya
4. Bhumij
5. Bhutia, Sherpa, Toto, Duka, Kagatay, Tibetan, Yolmo
6. Birhor
7. Birjia
8. Chakma
9. Chero
10. Chik Baraik
11. Garo
12. Gond
13. Gorait
14. Hajang
15. Ho
16. Karmali
17. Kharwar
18. Khond
19. Kisan
20. Kora
21. Korwa
22. Lepcha
23. Lodha, Kheria, Kharia
24. Lohara, Lohra
25. Magh
26. Mahali
27. Mahli
28. Mal Pahariya
29. Mech
30. Mru
31. Munda
32. Nagesia
33. Oraon
34. Parhaiya
35. Rabha
36. Santal
37. Sauria Paharia
38. Savar

ANDAMAN AND NICOBAR ISLANDS

[The Scheduled Castes and Scheduled Tribes Orders (Amendment) Act, 1976 (No. 108 of 1976, dated the 18th September, 1976)]

SCHEDULED TRIBES

1. Andamanese, Chariar, Chari, Kora, Tabo, Bo, Yere, Kede, Bea, Balawa, Bojigiyab, Juwai, Kol
2. Jarawas
3. Nicobarese
4. Onges
5. Sentinelese
6. Shom Pens

ARUNACHAL PRADESH

SCHEDULED CASTES

1. Bansphor
2. Bhuinmali or Mali
3. Brittial-Bania or Bania
4. Dhupi or Dhobi
5. Dugla or Dholi
6. Hira
7. Jalkeot
8. Jhalo, Malo or Jhalo-Malo
9. Kaibartta or Jaliya
10. Lalbegi
11. Mahara
12. Mehtar or Bhangi
13. Muchi or Rishi
14. Namasudra
15. Patni
16. Sutradhar

SCHEDULED TRIBES

All tribes of the Union Territory including :—

1. Abor
2. Aka
3. Apatani
4. Dafla
5. Galong
6. Khampti
7. Khowa
8. Mishmi
9. Momba
10. Any Naga tribes
11. Sherdukpen
12. Singpho

CHANDIGARH

SCHEDULED CASTES

1. Ad Dharmi
2. Bangali
3. Barar, Burar or Berar
4. Batwal
5. Bauria or Bawaria
6. Bazigar
7. Balmiki, Chura or Bhangi
8. Bhanjra
9. Chamar, Jatia Chamar, Rehgar, Raigar, Ramdasi or Ravidasi

10. Chanal
11. Dagi
12. Darain
13. Dhanak
14. Dhogri, Dhangri or Siggi
15. Dumna, Mahasha or Doom
16. Gagra
17. Gandhila or Gandil Gondola
18. Kabirpanthi or Julaha
19. Khatik
20. Kori or Koli
21. Marija or Marecha
22. Mazhabi
23. Megh
24. Nat
25. Od
26. Pasi
27. Perna
28. Pherera
29. Sanhai
30. Sanhal
31. Sansi, Bhedkut or Manesh
32. Sansoi
33. Sapela
34. Sarera
35. Sikligar
36. Sirkiband

DADRA AND NAGAR HAVELI

[The Constitution (Dadra and Nagar Haveli) Scheduled Castes Order. 1962, C.O. 64]

SCHEDULED CASTES

1. Bhangi
2. Chamar
3. Mahar
4. Mahyavanshi, Dhed

[The Constitution (Dadra and Nagar Haveli) Scheduled Tribes Order, 1962, C.O. 64]

SCHEDULED TRIBES

1. Dhodia
2. Dubla including Halpati
3. Kathodi
4. Kokna
5. Koli Dhor including Kolgha
6. Naikda or Nayaka
7. Varli

DELHI

[The Constitution (Union Territories, Scheduled Castes Order, 1951 C.O.32]

SCHEDULED CASTES

1. Adi-Dharmi
2. Agria
3. Aheria
4. Balai
5. Banjara
6. Bawaria
7. Bazigar
8. Bhangi
9. Bhil
10. Chamar, Chanwar Chamar,

Jatya or Jatav Chamar, Mochi, Ramdasia, Ravidasi, Raidasi, Rehgarh or Raigar
11. Chohra (Sweeper)
12. Chuhra (Balmiki)
13. Dhanak of Dhanuk
14. Dhobi
15. Dom
16. Gharrami
17. Julaha (Weaver)
18. Kabirpanthi
19. Kachhandha
20. Kanjar or Giarah
21. Khatik
22. Koli
23. Lalbegi
24. Madari
25. Mallah
26. Mazhabi
27. Meghwal
28. Naribut
29. Nat (Rana)
30. Pasi
31. Perna
32. Sansi or Bhedkut
33. Sapera
34. Sikligar
35. Singiwala or Kalbelia
36. Sirkiband

GOA, DAMAN & DIU

[The Constitution (Goa, Daman & Diu) Scheduled Castes Order, 1968, C.O. 81]

SCHEDULED CASTES

	Synonym
1. Bhangi	Hadi
2. Chambhar	
3. Mahar	
4. Mahyavanshi	Vankar
5. Mang	

[The Constitution (Goa, Daman & Diu) Scheduled Tribes Order, 1967]

SCHEDULED TRIBES

	Synonym
1. Dhodia	
2. Dubla	Halapati, Talavia
3. Naikda	
4. Siddi	Nayaka
5. Varli	

LAKSHADWEEP

[The Constitution (Union Territories) Scheduled Tribes Order, 1951, C.O. 33]

SCHEDULED TRIBES

Inhabitants of the Laccadive, Minicoy and Amindivi Islands who, and both of whose parents were born in those islands.

MIZORAM

SCHEDULED CASTES

1. Bansphor
2. Bhuinmali, Mali
3. Brittial Bania, Bania
4. Dhupi, Dhobi
5. Dugla, Dholi
6. Hira
7. Jalkeot
8. Jhalo, Malo, Jhalo-Malo
9. Kaibartta, Jaliya
10. Lalbegi
11. Mahara
12. Mehtar, Bhangi
13. Muchi, Rishi
14. Namasudra
15. Patni
16. Sutradhar

SCHEDULED TRIBES

1. Chakma
2. Dimasa, Kachari
3. Garo
4. Hajong
5. Hmar
6. Khasi, Jaintia, Synteng, Pnar, War, Bhoi, Lyngngam
7. Any Kuki Tribes, including :—
   (i) Biate, Biete
   (ii) Changsan
   (iii) Chongloi
   (iv) Doungel
   (v) Gamalhou
   (vi) Gangte
   (vii) Guite
   (viii) Hanneng
   (ix) Haokip, Haupit
   (x) Haolai
   (xi) Hengna
   (xii) Hongsungh
   (xiii) Hrangkhwal, Rangkhol
   (xiv) Jongbe
   (xv) Khawchung
   (xvi) Khawathlang, Khothalong
   (xvii) Khelma
   (xviii) Kholhou
   (xix) Kipgen
   (xx) Kuki
   (xxi) Lengthang
   (xxii) Lhangum
   (xxiii) Lhoujem
   (xxiv) Lhouvun
   (xxv) Lupheng
   (xxvi) Mangjel
   (xxvii) Misao
   (xxviii) Riang
   (xxix) Sairhem
   (xxx) Selnam
   (xxxi) Singson
   (xxxii) Sitlhou
   (xxxiii) Sukte
   (xxxiv) Thado
   (xxxv) Thangngen
   (xxxvi) Uibuh
   (xxxvii) Vaiphei
8. Lakher
9. Man (Tai speaking)
10. Any Mizo (Lushai) tribes
11. Mikir
12. Any Naga tribes
13. Pawi
14. Synteng

PONDICHERRY

[The Constitution (Pondicherry) Scheduled Castes Order, 1964, C.O.68]

SCHEDULED CASTES

1. Adi Andhra
2. Adi Dravida
3. Chakkiliyan
4. Jambuvulu
5. Kuravan
6. Madiga
7. Mala, Mala Masti
8. Paky
9. Pallan
10. Paryan, Sambavar
11. Samban
12. Thoti
13. Valluvan
14. Vetan
15. Vettiyan

3

PROBLEMS OF TRIBAL PEOPLES

The tribals of India occupy a unique position in Indian culture and civilization. They vary in number from 09 to lakhs and are varied in terms of their social, economic, cultural, religious, political systems etc. However, our main concern here is to discuss their problems. Their problems can be viewed in terms of (1) Felt problems and (2) Assessed problems. Felt problems are those which they feel and explain and the Assessed problems are those which are assessed and projected by the planners, bureaucrats, policy makers, anthropologists and such others as are involved and are instrumental in their development. The problems which we are going to discuss are mainly based on the assessed problems. Therefore they are diagnostic and prescriptive in nature.

Land Alienation

Tribal farmers occupy marginal lands of the areas in which they live and practice outmoded methods of farming, with the result that they produce at their fields barely sufficient to meet their own farm and family requirements. Subsistence sector of Indian agriculture therefore is to a good extent composed of tribal farms. How and why the tribals have turned into resourceless paupers and landless labourers is partly a sad story of their innocence and honesty and largely the story of their exploitation by the so-called more advanced section of the larger society. Dhebar commission has repeatedly stressed in its report to allot cultivable land of forest to tribals and to issue patta to grant secured rights in such lands. Most of the tribals are either small peasants possessing uneconomic holdings or cultivators cum tenants cum labourers. The trend of alienation of their land in favour of non-tribal people despite all out efforts of the State Governments and Union territories could not be arrested.

In tribal India land is used for (1) Forest-Fallow cultivation, (2) Bush fallow cultivation, (3) Short fallow cultivation, (4) Annual cropping and (5) Multi cropping.

Tribal cultivators have very low mobility therefore they continue to stay out at one place or are likely to shift within a specified area ; physical and social isolation have in the past allowed the tribals to keep their culture intact and bestowed upon them free living under their closed economy governed largely by their kinship ties and social orders. Isolation therefore had proved a boon. But this is not all ; so far as it saved them from their exploitation by the intruders, it was a boon. So far as it disallowed them the fruits of sciences and technologies and close link with the non-tribal world it proved to be a curse. Land has always been considered a community wealth for purpose of cultivation and its development.

With the opening of railways and road linking to remote cities and passing through the tribal areas, the tribals came into contact with middlemen, businessmen, forest and road contractors etc. The Govt. officials were the first to come in close contact of the tribals and so also the first exploiters. By and large the trade potentials also were explored with the improvement of means of transport and communications. The manufactured articles as well as money started flowing into tribal economy. With the result raw materials including forest produce and agricultural produce started flowing out as payment in kinds to areas of economic concentration. Land so far was not treated as a state-saleable commodity, but, it soon became saleable and transferable during the British regime. The exploitation of tribal cultivators thus started by transfer of their land to non-tribals or outsiders, who found it very favourable to settle down in remote interior areas having abundant land and human resources. Indebtedness of tribal folk had encouraged the bonded labour system that was developed with the passage of time through land alienation. Exchange economy gradually was transformed into a money oriented economy, related largely by the cash transactions and forward trading. This had expedited the transfer of land from tribal to non-tribals.

New excise laws and rules which had disallowed the tribals to extract liquor in their homes for self consumption soon led to tribals to fall in the traps of liquor contractors. They had been working as moneylender and rich agriculturists side by side to working as a liquor suppliers. This, however, was a half story of what helped and encouraged the land alienation of tribals. The other half runs into displacement of tribals among others, from their land as a result of construction of road, railways, public projects, factories etc.

The new uses of land has further deepened this problem. The irrigation development schemes and projects has aggravated the land alienation. The power projects meant for irrigation has displaced the tribals. Industries being located in tribal areas has also caused the land alienation. Measures to be taken to improve the situation are suggested below.

Having regard to the existing situation and the importance of the matter we recommend that :

1. The existing laws relating to transfer of land belonging to scheduled tribes should continuously be reviewed to plug the loopholes.
2. The areas of high incidence of land alienation in each state should be identified and suitable remedial measures taken on a time bound basis.
3. In areas where land restoration work is sizeable, adequate machinery should be created to settle the issues expeditiously.
4. Necessary inputs to develop the restored land should from a part of the developmental programmes.
5. Formal records of rights of tribals over land must be prepared within a time frame.
6. The progress of restoration of land should be reviewed regularly at the state and national levels.

Solution

The solution of this problem calls for three basic measures :

1. Legislative measures to stop it ;
2. Awakening or consciousness ; and
3. To restore the ownership of land to tribals with necessary legal support.

Planning Commission's Task Force on Agrarian Relation has suggested for debt redemption. To solve it the Scheduled Areas and Scheduled Tribes Commission (1961) popularly known as Dhebar Commission was constituted. Prior to it Backward Classes Commission was set up. In 1969, a study team on tribal development programmes were commissioned. In 1986, a task force committee has also been constituted by the Planning Commission to solve this and other allied problems of the tribals of India.

Bihar

Bihar is the third largest tribal state of India. Tactics of the traders and money lenders led to the dispossession of lands and consequent Santhal Rebellion of 1855. In Bihar therefore, four tenancy Acts are in force :

1. The Bihar Tenancy Act 1855.
2. The Chotanagpur Tenancy Act 1908.
3. The Santhal Parganans Tenancy (supplementary provision Act 1949.
4. The Ranchi district Tana Bhagat Rajput Agricultural Restoration Act 1947.

Apart from above to check the land alienation and to restore the land of the tribals a bill has been passed in March 1986 by the State Legislature.

Indebtedness

Ordinarily indebtedness reflects imbalances in relation to four factors. They are :

1. Resource deterioration, stagnation in technology and consumption leading to a production relation marked by intensive exploitation.
2. Rapid technological change without change in the quantum of total resources and the consumption pattern.
3. Stagnation in production relations as well as resource position but rapid change in the technology and consumption pattern leading to a vulnerable social structure marked by progressive pauperisation or displacement of a large segment of population.
4. Stagnation in resource position technology and production relations, but rapid change in consumption pattern.

However, the indebtedness has remained a difficult problem faced by the tribals of India. The tribals are widely exploited on account of indebtedness. It is due to their pauper status and impecunious condition. The earlier ethnographic accounts suggest that the tribals were not in the grip of money lenders when they were living in isolated state. We have no systematic and scientific anthropological account of the extent of indebtedness at all India level, however, we are concerned about the magnitude of the indebtedness among the tribals of India. Among tribals indebtedness has become unavoidable and the normal phenomenon of existence. Apart from the above mentioned causes of indebtedness, following may also be counted as the causes of indebtedness :

1. Loss of tribal rights over land and forest.
2. Poor and primitive mode of agriculture resulting in deficit supply of food grains.
3. Ignorance.
4. Expenditure beyond their means owing to their socio-eco-religious conditions.

Owing to the above factors no programme of economic development is likely to make its impact on the tribals from the clutches of the money lender. The tribals not only borrow in cash but in kind also. Munda and Oraon of Chotanagpur generally borrow seeds and rice during loan period and return four times more than what has been borrowed. The creditor, among Paharias, purchase the crop, fruit, bamboo etc. at very low rates in one, two or three years in advance.

Role of Money Lenders

The money lenders lend money without any formalities and just at the nick of time causing failure of all developmental programmes of the Government. To illustrate it, we will discuss the case of Sauria Paharia (Narayan 1986) : The Mahajans play a vital role as the Sauria Paharia are more or less in the habit of taking loan from them. They take loan at the time of cutting jungle, sowing, harvesting, marriage, death and during religious ceremonies. The Paharias themselves admit that once they take loan from the Mahajans it is difficult to free themselves from their debt because the interest goes on multiplying every year. Fifty per cent interest is taken on cash loan while hundred per cent is charged for the loan given in kind. During the period from November through February, which is harvesting season in the Paharia country, a man on horse back going towards the hills is a common sight. They are no other than Mahajans who after collection, return from the village with bags full of maize, millet, mustard etc. They take these grains at the current market price weighing them from a wooden measure called 'paila' (half seer measure). The price of the grain thus calculated is deducted from the amount of loan given to the Paharias. While returning from the village, they usually inform the Paharias that a certain amount of money still remained outstanding. It is impossible for a Paharia to understand the accounting. In spite of all these, the Mahajans are popular because they give loans quickly. The little land that they possess is still cultivated, in majority of the cases, by the Santhal or the Hindu Mahajans (p. 41-42).

Impact of Indebtedness

Since most of the tribals are illiterate they have no idea of what is being maintained in the Bahi (accounts register) of the money lenders. They give their thumb impression very obediently wherever required by the money lenders and that seals their fate for their future and for the future of the coming generations. In many cases such deals are oral and owing to their simplicity and bad economic condition are unable to approach the court of law. But even those transactions which are recorded on the accounts register are nothing but the legal fiction because of the wrong entries of inflated amounts. At the most, these cases are taken to their traditional panchayat which invariably would serve the purpose of the money lenders. Microstudies of the tribal India demonstrate that in most of the cases indebtedness leads to bondedness and land alienation. It results into :—

1. Slavery, bonded labour and free labour to the Mahajans.
2. Alienation of the land and its acquisition by Mahajans.
3. Sex exploitation and prostitution.
4. Chronic veneral and allied diseases, malnutrition etc.
5. The Sauria Paharias of Bihar are the classical example.

Legislations and Constitutional steps

1. The fifth schedule of the constitution empowers the Governor of a state to regulate the conduct of the business as money lender by persons who lend money to members of scheduled tribes in scheduled Area. In pursuance of this provision various state governments have promulgated and enacted various laws and Acts. Following are some of the important Regulations and enactment from different states to control money lending, debt redemption and abolition of debt bondages :

1. The Bihar State Scheduled Areas Money lenders Regulation 1985.
2. The Andhra Pradesh Scheduled Areas Money lenders regulation 1963.
3. The Assam Money lenders Regulation 1968.
4. The Bihar Money lenders (Regulation of Transaction) Act 1939.
5. The Bombay Agricultural Debtor's Relief Act 1947.
6. The Kerala Money lending Act 1958.
7. The Madhya Pradesh Anusuchit Janjati Rinisahayata Act 1966.

8. The Madras Indebted Agriculturist (Repayment of Debt) Act 1955.
9. The Mysore Pawn Brokers Act 1961.
10. The Orissa Money Lenders (Application of certain Provision) Regulation 1950.
11. The Rajasthan Sagri system Abolition Act 1961.

The data supplied by various agencies and voluntary organisations disclose that despite regulations the exploitation of tribal people has continued unabated. The Mahajans have taken very little note of the above legislations. The report of the Scheduled Tribes Commission and Planning Commission's Report of the Task force committee on Tribal Development Programmes support and this findings such state of affairs continues because of :

(i) The state governments have not made adequate use of the protective provisions of the Fifth Schedule of the Indian Constitution.

(ii) The state governments have not been able to make effective use of the penal provisions in their existing legislation against Mahajans.

3. Lack of will and commitment of all reasons are most responsible for the continued exploitation of the tribals by the greedy money lenders.

It is evident from the foregoing discussion that merely legislations and various enactments are not in themselves sufficient to solve the problem of indebtedness rather it is the 'real will' at various levels of development projects to minimise and to arrest the problems of indebtedness.

Lack of Educational facilities

The tribals, in general, have lived in isolated places. Their mode of economy is quite primitive. They had their own education system suiting to their needs. They did not have formal education until independence and enactment of Indian constitution for the development of the scheduled Tribes. The adoption of the constitution gave special right to the state as well as the central government for the promotion of formal education among scheduled tribes of India.

The growth of formal education among the tribal population in India may be viewed in the light of the facts yielded from census data. The census data of 1931 disclosed that only 0.7 percent of the tribal people were literate. This rose to 11 per cent in 1981 against 36 per cent for the entire population. The literacy rate among tribal women is obviously much lower. Thus the growth rate of literacy among the tribals is disappointing since independence barring a few tribes of north-easthern region like the Khasi, the Garo etc, who are benefited due to the network of the Christian missionary institutions.

In one of my very recent study (Dimensions of Develoment in Tribal Bihar, 1986), I have discussed the educational scene in Tribal Bihar under Traditional system and Modern system.

Traditional System

Under traditional system I have emphasised that "The Oraon of Chotanagpur had their own traditional institutions for imparting education to its young ones. Dhumkuria known as Joinkherpa in their language, is the youth dormitory for boys. Similarly youth dormitory for girls is popularly and locally known as Pe Erpa."

"Oraon boys were admitted to the membership of the Dhumkuria at about eight years of age. The membership of Dhumkuria was compulsory. The Dhumkuria boys were divided into three age groups, known as 'Turs'. The duration of membership for the first two groups was three years and for the older members till they got married. The Dhumkuria boys were also known as Dhangars and the girls as Pelos."

"The supervision and control of the dormitory was in the hands of Dhangar Mahto. The eldest among the boys was selected as Dhangar Mahto by the village council, and the ablest and the senior most among the girls, preferably a widow, was appointed as Barki-Dhangin, the leader of the girls. The appointment is for three years. The Dhangar Mahto was assisted by another called Chalaba or Kotwars. The duty of the Dhangar Mahto was to instruct the Dhumkuria boys in their social and religious duties. The Kotwar apart from assisting the Dhangar Mahto had to attend Jatras and dances and see that the boys and the girls turn up properly dressed and fully decked with flower and fineness for the occasion, and to compel each member to participate in the dance. If a member disobeys him he punishes him or her by beating with a plaited straw whip. If a Kotwar is absent from his duties he was liable to be fined by the Dhangar Mahto. Thus a strict discipline was maintained in the Dhumkuria.

"The new members were admitted only once in three years, and there were elaborate ceremonies of initiation. S.C. Roy has described the new moon hunt which precedes this and the taking by the women of the new pots of the water. The older boys decide which members to admitt into Dhumkaniya fraternity. On admission the parents have to supply as tuition fees, a lamp, a small earthen pot, fuel and enough oil to lighten the dormitory for a fortnight.

"The Dhumkaria boys had many social duties. They cooked for visitors at a wedding when the strangers came to the village and were accommodated in the dormitory. The Dhanjars had to attend to them, entertain them and wash their feet. The younger boys had to do the most work. Apart from serving the guests they had to serve the older boys, keep the Dhumkuria house well provided with fuel and to keep the hall clean".

"If a villager was in need of labour for thatching a house or for some other purpose he may apply to the Dhangar Mahto who was arranging with the boys to work for him. In return for their services they were either paid in cash or given a feast. If a cash was received it was generally spent on purchasing some new musical instruments or other requisites such as cloth for making flags etc, for the Dhumkuria. The boys had to perform special rites during epidemics'.

"There was a separate institution for the girls called the Peierpa in Barambe. It was open only to its members and its whereabouts was kept secret and only the Dhumkaria boys were supposed to know. The organisation and function was similar to that of Jonkherpa, as both the institutions were closely connected. The girls too were divided into three age groups and the duration of membership was the same. The supervision and the control of the maidens dormitory was in the hands of an elderly male Oraon known as Pelekotwar who was appointed by the elders of the village. He was responsible for any scandal that may occur in connection with the girls and he was fined by the village council for negligence of his duties.

"The duties of the maidens were similar to those of the Dhangars. They had to pound rice and make cakes at the weddings. When any body required the services of the girls for reaping or transplanting, he was applying for their pachcha service to the Borki Dagrin and the payment was made in cash or kind. In addition, each maiden was required to plant a strip of palm leaf mats as long as the length of bachelors' hall. These strips were stitched together into two or three mats and presented to the bachelors dormitory. These mats serve as beds for the boys and are renewed annually".

"The life in Dhumkuria used to begin early at night. After the round for formal salutation, dancing began at the village Akhara and continued till midnight. The members then disperse and go to their respective dormitories. Both the boys and girls dance together and freely mix with each other. This develops into intimate associations, but such companionship seldom ends in marriage'.

"The Dhumkuria thus has educational, economic and other public functions. The participation of the members of the Dhumkuria in various ceremonies and rituals like hunting, festivals and Jatra festivals is important. An Oraon child learns folksongs, folktales and tribal customs in this very institution. By participating in the agricultural operations of the different individuals of village as a member of Dhumkhuria provide a chance, insight and training for becoming a good farmer. The child enters with initiation into manhood and continue till marriage. They fulfil those integrative tasks which are beyond the scope of family and descent groups. Thus the Oraon society by recruiting all the members of the village community into the Dhumkuria fraternity seeks to extend the individual relations throughout the village community, irrespective of kinship affiliation.

"The above description of the Dhumkhuria suggest the ideal

role and functioning of the traditional institution. The Dhumkhuria of upper Tola exists only in name whereas the Dhumkuria of the Lower Tola is for ceremonial occasions. For some time the Dhumkuria of Upper Tola was used as a centre for night school by the members of Ramkrishna mission. The Oraon in general are unhappy over the current status and condition of Dhumkuria. They all want to revive it but none have money to contribute to maintain the Dhumkhuria even in present condition. They are of the opinion that when they do not have to eat then how can they think of maintaining Dhumkuria. They realised that the money being spent on rice is sufficient to maintain the traditional institution but they also admitted their inability to give up drinks. The Dhumkuria of Upper Tola is being used as meeting place of adult Oraons. It is also being used on ceremonial occasions like marriage, panchayat, etc.

"Dhumkuria of Lower Tola is being used by the Oraon of this Tola as a ceremonial institution. Whenever a visitor comes to the village they charge Rs. 50/- minimum and Rs.500/ maximum to show that Dhumkuria is still alive and is in action in the village. Members of this Dhumkuria also go to participate in various cultural and national programmes.

"In the traditional system, education was imparted by the Dhumkuria at the period of transition from childhood to adult life. The indigenous system was designed to train a child for group life and consequently attention was focused on the group rather than the individual (p. 13-16)."

Modern system

"The modern system of education has a wide scope for personal development. Under the changing circumstances Oraons realise that a wide world is open to them and it is no longer possible to mould a child exclusively for the tribal environment. They want education but they have strong limitations.

"Apart from informal education the Oraon of Barambe have the facilities of formal education. Such facilities of formal education are extended to them through the institutions formed by government or by missionaries. However, the response to such facilities is very poor.

"The Christian Oraon of Barambe are comparatively more educated than Hindu Oraon and former are concerned for the education of their childern whereas latter are not at all concerned about this. 6.2% of the total male population of the village are literate and 2.1% of the total female population of the village are literate.

"Christian missionaries were pioneers in the field of women's education. In the district co-education is a common feature in all primary schools. The children of the scheduled Tribes receive the same education as those of the non-tribals. They get all facilities from the state, on paper viz., full free studentship, book grant, stipend etc. In practice they are charged nominal fee by the concerned teacher and the book grant usually does not come to the school.

"There is one such school in the village. The figures displayed by the Government officials show that the number of schools, number of students and number of teachers have just doubled from 1951 till to date. It is not true with Barambe village. The school going Oraon childern in general and school teacher in particular feel that the facilities extended to them are inadequate and in some cases these facilities are not reaching them. The Oraon parents in general feel that even after 31 years of independence they are neglected.

"Unfortunately even today Barambe does not have a middle school in the village, such children of Barambe as desire to continue further education will have to cover the distance of 6 km. (one way). Similarly those who wish to pursue the high school education or further higher education will have to cover further more and more distance'.

"The rate of dropouts is higher. They admit their children in class I but due to economic problems, they cannot pursue their education. Similarly the total number of students of R.C. Mission school, Barambe also suggest the gradual dropouts in the total number of students. The teacher of the Mission School was also of the opinion that due to practical and real problems, the children admitted in Class I are not in a position to continue their education in Class II, III and even in IV.

N.N. Vyas and N.D. Chaudhuri (1971) while studying the extent and magnitude of dropouts and stagnation at various levels of education among scheduled tribes, scheduled castes and general students of Rajasthan are also of the opinion that 'The Percentage of dropouts was more in scheduled tribes boys compared to stagnation in all the session'. The total number of students remain constant in the end of the year, they have sufficient food to eat during the period but it fluctuates in between. The Government primary school does not suggest any dropouts during the class years whereas R. C. Mission school suggest dropout during the class year. Government schools are concerned with scholarship amount and the worth of the higherups of the office, therefore, they do not suggest any dropout during the class year.

"Oraon of Barambe in general were of the opinion that they had sufficient food to eat in the months of October, November, December and January and for rest of the period they hardly get one square meal. Children are considered economic asset of the family and therefore parents were of the opinion that except the above months they are not in a position to send their children to school as they help the family economy. Even during these months majority of them feel difficulty in sending their children to school.

"Children going to primary school of Barambe said that they have to obey their parents. Initially they are asked to take the cattle of the family to nearby forest, to look after their younger siblings, to help the parents in ploughing and sowing the land and in harvesting the paddy etc. They are engaged in such works from the very beginning so they develop a kind of taste for such work. When a few of them are asked to attend the school they feel bad because the rest of their friends are already working as the helping hand of their father. Oraon children also dislike going to school because by going so they do not get a chance to sing their folksongs with friends in a forest or lonely place etc". (Ibid p. 17-23).

What is true for Oraon is also true for other tribes of India. The following measures were recommended for enhancing the primary education :

1. Holding the school in the evening.
2. Making reading materials available to them free of cost.
3. Mid-day meals should be served to attract the students and their parents. This will also minimise the disease growing out of hunger.
4. The school should be located in Dhumkuri. It will serve two purposes i.e. Dhumkuri will be maintained and due to its central location in the village childr-ı will have no difficulty in attending the school.
5. The teachers should not only be tribals but should also have necessary zeal and aptitude for the development of their own brethren.
6. Non formal education may also be fruitfully tried among them.

Similarly the working group on the tribal development during Seventh Plan suggest : "we feel that while the cor economic sector might hold primacy in planning, education is the key to tribal development. The tribal segment of the society is placed in a position of handicap vis-a-vis the non tribal sections as it has little access to education and, hence knowledge of the modern affairs. The isolation of the tribal communities has limited their world view severely and in dealing with the present day administration systems like law courts, police, revenue, forest, money lending, trading etc., they find themselves incapable. Education is, therefore, an input noe only for economic development but also for inner strength of tribal communities so that they can meet the new challenge on terms of some degree of equality."

Education has to be tackled on both the non-formal and formal levels.

Since it is a concurrent subject, the connected problems should engage the attention of both the central and state authorities. A substantial programme of non-formal education and citizenship training has to be mounted in order to disseminate widely among the scheduled tribe people knowledge and information which should enable them face confrontation with non-tribal forces. In the non-formal education programme organised by the Ministry of Education, coverage of tribal areas and enrolment of member of scheduled tribes have been given a high priority. These need to be quantified. But apart from mere numbers, the preparation of curricula and reading material need perceptive and sensitive handling by both the central and state agencies. The course content should include instruction as to how to deal with problems connected with land, credit, currency, weights and measures, hygiene, local geography, local administration, lower government functionaries, liquor vendor etc. Organisational efforts should be looked into carefully. Periodical evaluation of the programme should enable a plateau of continued optimality.

On the formal education side also, both the qualitative and quantitative aspects should engage serious attention. The current conventional syllabi might not suit children of the tribal communities. Steps should be taken to work out syallabi for education taking into account their culture, technology, ethos and assimilative power. The new syllabi should not, however, place the tribal students in any position of disadvantage with reference to entry into higher educational institutions or employment. At the national level, the Ministry of Education, the National Council of Educational Research and Training, the National Institute of Educational Planning and administration might set up a body to evolve broad guidelines for imparting the requisite orientation to the conventional system. But since there is considerable variation in the socio-cultural background even among the various scheduled tribe communities in a state, the content and bias may have to differ from one tribe to another. The question of evolving relevant courses of study for the various tribes should receive the earnest attention of State Education Department, the Tribal Development Department and the State Institute of Education.

Article 350 lays down that it shall be the endeavour of every state and of every local authority within the state to provide adequate facilities for instruction in the mother tongue at the primary stage of education to children belonging to linguistic minorities groups.

By the end of seventh plan period at least 5% of schools in tribal areas in a state should run primary classes as per the revised syllabi.

In an adequate number of the usual educational institutions, vocational facilities should be provided i.e. agriculture training, industrial trades, sports etc. so that services become actually available to the tribal. The pattern of education should be linked with job opportunities.

Inability on the part of the members of scheduled tribe communities to utilise secondary and higher education facilities as well as job opportunities in full can partly be explained by defects in their education at the successive lower tiers. For example, it has been reported that the tribal boys and girls are not able to gain entry into ITIs and other technical Institutes due to their weakness in science learning. In order to overcome it, science teaching should be strengthened in the middle and the high schools. For science teaching and coaching in other concerned subjects, special classes outside the school hour be held for which result linked honorarium may be paid to teachers.

In the field of employment, absence of contacts, in fact absence of nexus between tribal areas and the concerned urban centres, stands in the way of exploitation of employment potential. Employment exchanges seem to have been established in certain tribal areas without much results. Vocational guidance centres should be set up in these areas so that tribal boys and girls get sound advice regarding their ability and quantifications vis-a-vis job opportunities. Such centres will promote utilisation of employment facilities.

Low enrolment ratio, sparseness of educational institutions serving tribal habitations, high wastage rate, absentee teachers are some of the features of educational programmes in tribal areas. Some of them stem from the economic status of the tribals, some from neglect in establishment of educational institutions and some others from lack of facilities for government employees obtaining in the tribal areas. We feel that all these need attention.

Pre-matric and post-matric scholarships are being disbursed by the states to students belonging to scheduled tribe communities. There have been complaints of delay in disbursement, so much so that on account of late availability of the first installment some students have been unable to join the institutions as they have no funds to make advance payment of the initial fees, caution money, hostel dues etc. The scholarship amounts should be disbursed in advance in order to meet such contingencies, with appropriate safeguards.

The norms for establishment of educational institution at the primary, middle and secondary level need to be scrutinised once again to ensure their relevance for tribal areas particularly on account of the facts that the density of population is low and habitants are spread far apart. The structural balance among the primary, middle and secondary institutions should be properly struck and maintained. The problem of remoteness and inaccessibility can be overcome by decentralisation of the educational institutions and hostels.

Multiplicity of governmental organisations running educational institutions might be rationalised. Coordination with Education Department should be ensured by the concerned organisations.

One of the major constraints in the expansion of educational programme is finance. Large investment in Pucca buildings curtail the programmes. Further limited and delayed availability of construction material like cement, iron rods etc. acts an effective brakes. At the same time, it has been found that in case of certain tribal communities, modern structures run counter to the grain of tradition and sensibility of the children of those tribes. With a view to effect economy in construction and harmony of environment, indigenous material and specifications, with such refinement as may be necessary, may be adopted.

I strongly feel that a sound monitoring system should be set up from the grass-roots level through state to national level. There is a need in fact to appoint in the State Directorates of Education specific officers in the rank of Joint Director or Deputy Director to specifically attend to the problems of education among scheduled tribes and to monitor data.

Shifting Cultivation

Shifting cultivation occupies a distinct place in the tribal economy. It constitutes a vital part of the socio-economic network of tribal life. Shifting cultivation may be defined as an agricultural system which is characterized by a rotation of field rather of crop, by short period of cropping (one to three years) alternating with long fallow periods (up to twenty and more years) but often as short as six to eight years and by clearing by means of slash and burn (Pelzer, 1958). As Conklin explains "shifting cultivation implies an aimless, unplanned, nomadic movement or an abrupt chance in location, either of which may refer to the cropping areas, the agriculturists or both. Aside from being ambiguous and in many case inaccurate, these implication do not focus attention on the two most widely shared characteristics of these various systems; firing and fallowing". However, making it more precise in a recent minimal definition Conklin described shifting cultivation "as an agricultural system in which fields are cleared by firing and are cropped discontinuously".

Basic features

The minimal definition of shifting cultivation reflects its real value. However, a single definition does not appear to be wide enough to touch upon all its essential aspects. Firing of the wood and discontinuous cropping by shifting of the plot are two gross morphological criteria which could be used as most significant and useful diagnostic elements in the analysis of shifting cultivation.

1. Practised chiefly by simpler cultures or small total population but occasionally used by almost any one to whom the cropping system appears expedient.
2. Human labour chiefly in operation, using a few hand tools primarily, but power tools are used occasionally.
3. Labour pattern frequently co-operational, but involving many variations in working group structure.
4. Clearing of fields primarily by felling, cutting, slashing and burning and using fire to dispose of vegetation debris, after drying in special situations fire may not be used.
5. Frequent shifting of cropped fields, normally in some kind of sequence in land control, resting in special social groupings under customary law, but sometimes occurring under other legal institutions of land control.

6. Many different systems in crop planting in given fields but both multiple cropping and specialized cropping present.
7. Use of annual and short term food crops predominant, but important use of long term shrub and tree crop is common.
8. Use of crops primarily for subsistence but admitting that exchange patterns may reach total sale of whole product.
9. Fields per acre and per man hour normally compared with those of permanent field agriculture within regions in which comparison is properly made but yields are often below those of mechanically powered permanent field agriculture.
10. Small annual cropped area per capita but comparable to that of the other no-powered sedentary cropping systems.
11. Use of vegetatian cover as soil conditioner and source of plant nutrient for cropping cycle.
12. When system is efficiently operated, soil erosions no greater than soil erosions under other system that are being efficiently operated.

Shifting cultivation in the country is practised primarily in seven states : Arunachal Pradesh, Assam, Manipur, Mizoram, Meghalaya, Nagaland and Tripura. It is practised partly in Bihar, Orissa, Andhra Pradesh, Madhya Pradesh and Kerala. There are some communities in Madhya Pradesh, Maharashtra, Karnataka and Sikkim who practice shifting cultivation marginally. It is reported that there are about 233 blocks spread over 62 districts in 16 states as the affected area under shifting cultivation set a higher or lesser degree involving nearly 12% of the tribal population of the country. Most of the areas under shifting cultivation have not been estimated on the basis of surveys and basic information like the actual area, exact location, population dependent on it, production, consumption, level of development etc. are not available.

Notwithstanding the deleterious effects of shifting cultivation on soil and water regime, it has been conceded that in the context of (a) the total absence of capital formation in tribal areas and (b) land man ratio being not unfavourable, it is not an unscientific method of cultivation. On the other hand, a higher pressure of population has led to shortening of the cycle of shifting cultivation with consequent diminution in the supportive capacity of a unit of land. The effects of prolonged shifting cultivation are starkly in evidence in certain areas like the Koraput district of Orissa, where the barren rounded reddish-brown hills are unable to grow even a blade of grass and the soil has been reduced to ferruginous laterite due to continual erosion. Ecologists and environmentalists are outraged at such vandalism and would like shifting cultivation to be banned altogether. While we are in sympathy with their deep concern, we cannot share the "ban" view from the essentially human view point of the tribals. The tribals have been used to this pattern of cultivation for ages and are attached to it where shifting cultivation is still practised, their life and culture have been woven around it as much as settled agriculture has determined item elsewhere. More or less, the tribal has been able to evolve harmony between technology and ritual in shifting cultivation. The shifting cultivation also draw attention to animal sacrifice ceremonies believed by tribals to promote fecundity. Shifting cultivation would therefore, appear to pose the problem : how to usher in technological advancement without alienating the tribal communities practising it.

We are aware that no single satisfactory answer has yet been evolved. In fact, we are constrained to observe that while piecemeal attempts have been made to study and tackle it and even some international organisations have shown interest, a comprehensive approach in study, research and application has yet to emerge. It has to be appreciated that an activity which comprehends food production, religious, social and economic systems of the tribals may not be amenable to compartmentalised, sectoral approach made individually and separately by foresters, agronomists, horticulturists, animal husbandry experts, educationists, health experts etc. But the need for integrated concept is no where so great as when we are dealing with tribal communities practicing shifting cultivation which have been placed only next to primitive tribal groups in the scale of socio-economic progress.

Forestry should be undertaken on hill tops, horticultural plantations in the intermediate slopes and terrace cultivation in the foot-hills. This may be acceptable as a very broad strategy, but evidently each contextual situation should be studied in detail and will rule its own imperatives. We would suggest institution of pilot rehabilitation schemes for typical situations, inclusive of rubber, coffee, tea and horticulture plantations. A definite proportion of the total outlay on agriculture and allied sectors in states having sizeable shifting cultivators should be allocated with an additional nucleus fund, in favour of the concerned project Administrations.

The need for integrated approach becomes clearer still when it is realised that for a group of persons displaced from its present occupational and living pattern, a well conceived viable alternative may have to consist of mixed agriculture, i.e. containing components of agriculture horticulture, irrigation, animal husbandry, forestry, even cottage industry. For such backward communities as under consideration, inputs of social services like education, health etc. would require to be added. In fact, provision of the basic or minimum needs would become an imperative necessity. The entire programme is to be executed as one synergistic package, requiring project approach. It is suspected that many earlier programmes for tackling the problem suffered due to lack of integrated, multidisciplinary approach.

The approach has to commence right from the stage of formulation of the project report for regulating shifting cultivation. There should be clear direction to rehabilitation of shifting cultivators.

There are areas in the country where the community orders land use and areas where individual ownership and enterprise hold away. We would not like to interfere with the traditional system. It is believed that it will be possible to carry out the aforesaid measures to regulate shifting cultivation within the existing social framework in the best interest of the individual family, the community and the ecology.

Migration

The tribal situation in the country presents a varied picture. Some areas have high tribal concentration, while some others have no tribal population at all. About 250 scheduled tribe communities speaking about 105 languages and 225 subsidiary languages are scattered along the length and breadth of the country, from the Himalayas to the Indian ocean and from the Arabian sea to the eastern frontiers. Amongst them are groups as large as about 5 million and as small as eleven. Each community, irrespective of its numbers has come to occupy a place of its own in national life, retaining its own identity and culture.

Tribal development is often taken to be synonymous with rural development. The nation has rather risky consequences and is not often realised that they vary widely in their level of socio-economic development, cultural background, personality, psyche, language etc. Each of these groups calls for a unique prescription for development.

Article 46 of the constitution enjoins on the state to promote with special care the educational and economic interests of the weaker sections of the people and in particular of the scheduled castes and the scheduled tribes and to protect them from social injustice and all forms of exploitation. Some other provisions enable the President to make arrangement for implementation of the objective set forth in Article 46. Article 244 empowers him to declare an area as a scheduled or tribal area under the Fifth schedule, the Governor has been vested with the authority to modify state and central laws and to make Regulations for the peace and good government of scheduled Areas. Article 339 (2) lays down that the executive power of the Union extends to the giving of directions to a state as to the drawing up and execution of schemes for the welfare of the scheduled tribes in the state. Further, paragraph 3 of part A of the Fifth Schedule provides that the executive power of the Union shall extend to the giving of directions to the state as to the administration of scheduled Areas. Article 275 provides for financial assistance to state for implementation of schemes of development of scheduled tribes and raising the level of administration in the Scheduled Areas. Article 15,

16 and 19 make it possible, while legislating on any matter, to take into consideration and special conditions of tribal in the matter of enforcing the provisions relating to equality of all citizens.

It would thus, appear that while the Scheduled Areas are to be administered as part of the State in which they are situated, wide powers have been conferred on the Governor for their administration. He has been enabled to modify Central and State laws in their application to them and to frame Regulations for the peace and good government and, in particular, for the protection of the rights of tribals in land and the allotment of waste land and their protection from the money lenders. He is required to consult the Tribes Advisory Council in the State in framing of these Regulations. Notwithstanding such powers, land alienation continues to take place, usury is rampant and incidence of bonded labour does not appear to have substantially abated.

The importance of migration in developing countries cannot be underestimated. It is a major factor in economic development and manpower planning, it has acquired special significance in the context of commercialization of agriculture, it has major implications for unbanization, slums and social change, it has notable feedback effects on the place of origin, as the migrants maintain different kinds and degree of contact. This important place that migration occupies in the social and cultural life of the people has not been commensurate with the attention it has so far received by anthropologists in our country.

Migration occurs more or less continuously over times. In order to study its incidence, data have to be compiled with reference to specified periods of time. This interval may be definite, e.g. the life time of the population alive at a given date. When the data refer to a definite interval we may say that they measure fixed term or period migration, and thus distinguish them from data on life time migration on data based on place of last residence that lack a definite time reference.

An out-migrant is a person who departs from migration defining area by crossing its boundary to a point outside it but within the same country. He is to be distinguished from an 'emigrant' who is an international migrant, departing to another country by crossing an international boundary. While migration excludes short visits and tours, it includes different types of both voluntary and involuntary movements. Examples of involuntary movements are migration under such crises as war, transfer of population, riots, floods, droughts and earthquakes. It also includes marriage migration, virilocal, uxorilocal or neolocal and transfer migration. There are other situations of migration where movement is part of people's earning a livelihood. These are nomads, shifting cultivators, itinerant traders and salesmen, artisans and labourers.

Historically, both internal and overseas migration have been associated with widespread military conquests, agricultural colonization and populations, expeditions of merchants, traders and religious missionaries, slave trade and indentured labour. These instances of migration currents provided the basis for early diffusionist, culture contact and acculturation theories.

Studies in migration stemmed from theoretical sources, culture contact theories and the Marxian analysis of colonization and alientation. While the former approach is dated, the latter is highly significant in studying the process of migration and its consequences in the capitalist mode of production. For instance colonization of tribal region in different parts of India, specially in Bihar, has led to conflicts between the migrants and the native tribes. Large scale exploitation of the benefits for scarce resources by the migrants has resulted in conditions of acute relative deprivation of the tribals. The perception of such conditions by the local tribes has led to militant messianic and millenarian movement. The problem of ethnicity has assumed an important place in migration studies specially in the urban contexts. The tribal ethnicity has currently assumed an important place and it needs to be studied on priority basis.

The foremost consequence of large scale migration of unskilled and semiskilled workers to the cities is the development of slums.

To what states do migrants move? According to 1961

census, the major flows have been to West Bengal (especially the industrial belts in the Hoogly and Damodar Valley regions) Maharashtra (greater Bombay and Poona), Punjab (the industrial towns along the railway lines between Amritsar and Delhi), Assam (the tea plantation), Mysore (the industrial complex around Bangalore and the gold fields at Kolar) and Madhya Pradesh (with the heavy electrical industries at Bhopal).

In terms of proportion of immigrants to total population, West Bengal and Punjab with 15.7 per cent and 14.2 per cent respectively are the leading states ; Assam comes next with 11.4 per cent of its population being migrants followed by Maharashtra with 7.3 per cent and the hill state of Himachal Pradesh with 6.6 per cent.

The growth of land alienation, the establishment of rent and money lending that called for cash income, and the gradual increase of the tribal population as the death rate declined, led to the emergence by the second half of the nineteenth century of a pool of surplus agricultural labourers.

In the middle of the nineteenth century the British were looking for a labour force they could recruit to work on their plantations in Assam and Bengal as tea pickers. The tribals of Chotanagpur were attractive recruits, they were 'surplus', i.e. they were in need of work ; they were accustomed to hard labour ; they were acclimated to the hill areas and the distances though substantial could be traversed by rail, road and steamer. British recruitment in Chotanagpur region began in the middle of the century, chiefly among the Santhals and the Mundas. The Santhals emigrated from Santhal Parganas and Manbhum and the Mundas from Ranchi and Hazaribagh.

If we take 1921 as the peak year of emigration, when slightly under a million tribals were living in Bengal, Assam and other parts of India, and when the tribal population of Chotanagpur was approximately three million, we can estimate that nearly a third of the tribal population had emigrated or to put the magnitude another way, had there been no out-migration of tribals, the tribal population of Chotanagpur and Santhal Parganas in 1971, taking into account natural population increases, would have been about six million instead of one and a half.

Actually, it is likely that the long-term demographic effects have been even greater than the numbers indicate, since the migrants were young tribals of child bearing age whose fertility would most probably have been higher than those who did not migrate.

There is no exclusive study on the outmigration of the tribals of Chotanagpur. However, the passing reference on the subject has been made in some recent studies. Sachchidananda in Changing Munda (1980) has mentioned that "since early 1970's there is a seasonal migration among the Mundas of Khunti area to Punjab where they work as agricultural labourers in the fields of rich peasants. They are recruited and transported by middleman styled as 'Sardars' on commission from the Munda labourers and their employers. The agricultural labourer from Chotanagpur is a cheaper substitute to his counterpart in Punjab. He is paid Rs. 60/- p.m. along with meals, clothing and living room. He is supposed to serve his Master for a period of six months which is the period of contract" (p. 150).

This has been corroborated by Manjit Singh and K. Gopal Iyer in their paper entitled "Migrant Labour for Green Revolution" (Voluntary Action, Vol. 24, No. 1) wherein they mention that "the early recruitment of tribals started towards the close of the sixties when some Punjabi farmers having links with Ranchi brought few tribals for personal work"

Munda, Santhal, Oraon, Ho etc., are the major tribes of Bihar. Apart from these there are some minor tribes also like Birhors, Malpaharia, Sauria Paharia, Kumarbhag, etc. The bulk of the outmigrants permanent or seasonal are from the major tribes for the reasons mentioned above.

Migration of tribals of Bihar to tea plantation of Assam, rural areas of Haryana, Punjab etc., industrial complex and urban areas of West Bengal, Bihar and to other states poses several specific problems for anthropological investigations. Their problem of adjustment are different from those of non-tribal labourers and peasants. There are both the problems of inter-tribal relations and the tribal and non-tribal relations in such cities that need to be studied besides their changing economic and property relations and family and religious life. N.C.

Chaudhary in his paper 'A Study on Tribal Migration. (1963) shows that tribes move in groups maintaining their ethnic identity.

Seasonal migration occupies a very important place in migration studies, but unfortunately it is the most neglected area. Since the census data are not useful in this regard, primary studies are needed to understand the different dimensions of the problem, inclnding working conditions, the role of middlemen, nature of exploitation and an assessment of relevant legislations. Seasonal migration has acquired a singular importance in the context of commercial crops. There are other operations which need seasonal labour such as bamboo cutting, felling of trees for timber, construction of road, brick work and other areas like desilting of tanks and canals and building tanks, bridges and dams. M.S.A. Rao (1981) has mentioned in his paper that contrary to the popular impression, seasonal migration is work specific and a certain group specializes in particular job.

Seasonality is relative to economic and social conditions of migrants at the place of origin and of destination. Seasonal migrants tend to be exploited by the middlemen and hence the process of recruitment and different patterns of organization of work needs to be studied in detail. Migration is also considered as an investment in human capital involving cost-benefit analysis at different levels.

Anthropological approach to migration has been built up over a period of years in bits and pieces since Marxian culture—contact and Revenstine's (1885) theories. Sachindra Narayan (1983) studied the overall impact of migration on the socio-economic life of the tribal Bihar, the causes and the ramifications.

Any study of migration should consider the historical development of the region, the wide economic and political conditions which regulate and condition the nature of employment opportunities. Scondly economic and social conditions at the place of origin need to be examined in order to understand why people move or do not move. At the individual level we have to consider not only the level of skills and family circumstances but the whole process of socialization and personality factors. It is important to realise that economic factors provide only the necessary conditions of migration, the sufficient conditions are the motivation to move, presence of resources networks and access to information flows. The latter make migration selection in terms of age, sex, marital status and the phase of development of the domestic group.

What happens to the migrants at the place of destination, their problem and process of settlement, employment, success and failure and their social organization are not entirely unrelated to their contacts with the place of origin. Hence the continuity interaction process between the place of origin and of destination is an essential aspect of migration studies.

Thus a large number of tribals migrates seasonally in search of work to distant places, particularly from those areas where the pressure of population is high and natural resources have got depleted. It is quite obvious that they comprise the weakest sections of the country. It will take sometime, may be a long time, before they can find adequate employment opportunities in and around their own villages. The interstate Migrant Workmen (Regulation of Employment and condition of Service) Act 1979 has been passed by Parliament to protect the interests of migrant labourers. It is understood that the Ministry of Home Affairs had proposed to the State Governments promulgation of a Regulation under the Fifth Schedule of the constitution for safeguarding the interest of tribal labour, particularly from the malpractices employed by contractors in Scheduled Areas where industries are located.

Forest and Tribe

Ancient India had a deep appreciation of the role of forest in making the earth a salubrious place to live This has sometimes taken the form of tree worship. There are innumerable references of this arboreal veneration in the scriptures and works by great Indian poets like Valmiki and Kalidas. Apart from this evocative aspects, they also had made intense studies of various plant species, their enormous food, nutritional and medicinal values and other uses. It is inconceivable how they did it but what they knew about the importance of the forest cover for maintaining soil fertility and productivity and its profound influence on climate specially rainfall, without the aid of any scientific tool will put a modern agronomist and agromolotytogist to share.

Pressure of population and sheer awareness prompted man to throw to winds this vast accumulated knowledge and experience in the last few decades. Since the beginning of the century, for example, the expanding human settlements had begun to encroach upon more and more forest areas and denude them of everything nature had evolved and built up for upwards of 50 million years. According to an estimate of the Food and Agriculture Organisation about 12 million hectares of forest cover is thus destroyed. Each year of this about 5 million are in Latin America and Asia and the remainder in Africa. India alone lost about 3-4 million hectares of forest, mostly in Bihar.

Tribals and forest have a very important role to play. Their traditional relationship with forests and trees, is largely based on a variety of goods and service they obtain from them and also due to the fact that trees and forests form a part of their environment and culture.

The present National forest policy adopted by the forest departments have proved inadequate. Upland exploitation of forest and their demolition, contains at an accelerated pace. Degradation of the environment and consequent ecological imbalance, have been brought about by excessive population pressure and ever declining resource base. Social tension is common in forest region, because there is inadequate participation of the peoples in the programme. Very little of the resources of forestry are available at the level of local community. There is greater urgency to develop dynamic system for forest management. Social forestry is an integral part of the total tribal development which aims at mobilizing the tribals to make self-reliant. Tribals need to be awakened about the new role of forests and must be sufficiently benefited from social forestry. The concept of social Forestry though not yet fully accepted as a doctrine, but concentrates on the publication and development of forest communities.

The beginning of state management of forest in mid-ninteenth century made deep inroads into the uses and benefits desired by tribals from forests. It marked the growing hiatus in perception towards forests or tribals on the one hand and forest authorities on the other.

The hitherto unfettered rights and privileges were regulated and restricted by the 1894 policy resolution of the government of India, the 1952 Resolution converted the "rights and privileges" into "rights and concessions", as observed by the Dhebar Commission. At the time of launching of the 1952 policy, it was averted that village communities in the neighbourhood of a forest wanted to make excessive use of its products for satisfaction of domestic and agricultural needs, but such use should not be permitted at the cost of national interests. This is really the heart of the matter. The management of forests and vegetable resource should be such as will provide for maximum goods and services for the well being of all sections of the country's population, there has to be judicious balance between the national needs such as defence, communications, industries etc. and the local, particularly tribal needs.

The forests are one of the main source of economic prosperity to tribals country. They also control soil erosion and provide food and fuel. Until last century the country had at least 30 per cent of its land under forest, but today, the percentage has gone further low. Bihar has a total forest area of 29,232 sq. km. constituting 16·8 per cent of the states land area as against the all India percentage of 23 per cent. The per capita forest area in Bihar is 0.05 hectare against the all India average of 0.14 hectare.

The Government acting on the recommendation of the National Commission on Agriculture, has finalised a scheme to raise social forestry through mixed plantation on common lands. Accordingly, the scope of the social forestry programme was defined to include farm forestry, extension forestry, reforestation of degraded forests and recreation of forestry. The State Government are being encouraged to implement the special social orestry programme with foreign assistance also. During the sixth plan (1980-85) a sum of Rs. 100 crores has been earmarked for these schemes. Of this, Rs. 50 crores will be provided by the Union Government towards centrally sponsored schemes to be implemented by State Government.

The projected demand of fuelwood in the country by 2000 A.D. is 225 million cu. m. according to the National commission on Agriculture. By the end of the fifth plan, plantations under farm forestry/firewood/social forestry schemes had been raised on an area of 1.5 million hectares. From these plantations 15 million cu. m. of fuelwood will be available per year on a 10 to 15 year rotation at the rate of 10 cu. m. per hectare per annum. Total availability of fuelwood by 1979-80 was about 18.5 million cu. m. including firewood from natural forests. This would still leave a gap of over 192 million cu. m. by the end of 200 A.D.

Forests are intimately connected with the life of tribals and plays a vital role in their economy. The relationship has been recognised but has not been defined and interpreted in terms of clear cut policies and programmes. This has caused adverse ecological balance. The history of tribals can be narrated in terms of changing relationship with the nature and forest. Early man acquired greater skills and in food gathering and hunting, with increased power of exploiting natural resources.

Forest conservancy began in tribal Bihar in 1946 when an area of 461 sq. km. of forests was demarcated to this endfor the first time in the history of Chotanagpur and Santhal parganas. According to 1971 census there were about five million tribals. The tribals have not yet reached a level of economic and industrial development adequate to assure them even a minimum measures of freedom from want. They depend mainly on forest resources for their livelihood. The forest is interwoven with their socio-religious-economic life. The nature of land, lack of irrigation and mode of cultivation hardly yield one squre meal for three months in a year. During the lean period they have to depend on forest products. Forest products are abused for construction for huts. Agricultural and hunting equipment are made from forest produce. Forest is closely linked with their festival. The sal tree is associated with Sarhul and Karma tree with Karma festival. Earlier, collection of wood was primarily of their own use, but now it has become important source of income during lean period to enable them to sustain against continuous hunger. Women collect not only fuelwood, but many other minor forest produce like mahua flower and seed, sal leaves and branches and fodder and which they sell in the nearby market to supplement their income. In the absence of alternative occupation they have to take whatever is available in forests.

Forestry has been essential throughout history for survival of tribal communities. During the pre-independence period the free use of forests and the liberty enjoyed by the tribals was curtailed through the imposition of restrictions by British Administrators. During post-independence era the policy of assessment of the forest resources in terms of modern economics had greatest blow on traditional tribal forest economy based on forest goods and service relations. This resulted in the forestry development into the resource developing and revenue earning activity. Initially, rights of tribals in forest were not challenged and tribal never felt bothered about these state of activities while the state may begin to assess its right, but the tribal still believes that the forest belongs to him. Some conflicting situation arises, when the state asserts its right through formal legal sanction. These rights have in course of time now become concessions in some cases, with further change of forest policies.

The rights and concessions for the tribals of Bihar have been defined and notified from time to time. The extension of rules of forest law and control which the forest staff exercised have considerably disturbed the tribal economy and have caused great resentment against the forest officials. With the gradual extension of the law regarding reservation and conservation of the rights of the tribals, people in the forests are now being restricted to mere concessions which means considerable hardship to them in getting their living. For this they are bound to exploit forest wealth and for which they suffer harassment at the hands of forest officials with the enforcement of forest laws, tribals have been deprived of forest produce, shelter and protection on the one hand, but are allured to encroach forest land for cultivation on the other.

Wood cutting, over-grazing and continuous destruction of forest resources lead to denudation. Non-tribals in the tribal belt are equally responsible for this situation. If deforestation persists with this pace, a day will come when firewood will be hardly available even for cooking one meal. Not only is the ecological balance affected but the tribals whose economy largely depends on forest will face difficulties. To uplift the tribals we have to improve their economic conditions and at the same time save and enlarge the forests. This means preserving, maintaining and improving the forests with all their resources, with the cooperation of the local tribals. The people's participation in forestry development will ensure that local community continues to have full command of the resources by inputs of forestry development. The social forestry programmes like roadside plantation, plantation on panchayat lands, tree farming, social security through plantation and development of private nursery, cost of manure and pesticides as also technical know-how etc. are some of the experimental programmes, to provide forestry an economic base. Gradually the programme can aim at increasing utilization of forest by the local community. Careful planning to link forest resources with the interest of the local economy should be the primary focus of the programme.

The tribal visualises the Forest Department as the greatest competitor in exploitation of forest, which they feel already belong to them. Much depends on the efforts made to take tribals into confidence and also on mode of persuasion. Individual tribal farmers becoming owners of the forest had to be induced to scientific management lest they should lose valuable assets. Tribals must have a feel that the programme is meant to strengthen their economy. They need to be trained in self management of forestry programme involvement of the local tribal and community participation is a pre-requisite for successful implementation of social forestry in tribal region of the country as a whole and in Bihar particularly. Their participation can be secured through voluntary agencies or by creating a cadre of extension services within the organisation. Their participation should be sought from policy formulation level to the level of execution. The successful implementation of the programme will enhance the economic condition of the tribals and will broaden the road of tribal development. It may also bridge the gap of "alien or stranger feeling" between tribals and the officials of Forest Department and also between tribals and non-tribals. If the programme is implemented in its true spirit that may also minimise the so-called "social tension" of the tribals region to a greater extent.

Unemployment

The unemployment is a new phenomenon in tribal India. When a tribal whether literate or illiterate, skilled or unskilled, does not get a job to earn his living it causes unemployment. With the growth in population and presence in tribal areas of non-tribals, there has been a net outflow of resources from many of the tribal areas leaving them impoverished. This is illustrated by instance of zones inhabited by the so-called primitive groups. One tends to presume that on account of the small numbers comprised in each of such groups, the proportion between natural resources and human beings would be favourable. This is not borne out from experience of such small communities as the Juang in the district of Keonjhor, the Kutti Kondh of the district of Phulbani (both of Orissa), the Sauria Paharia of the district of Sahebganj (Bihar), the Saharia of Rajasthan. Almost all such communities suffer from effect of undernourishment. Hence the foremost requirement is to give a boost to the production system of the trade concerned and at the same time, to provide off season employment for means of sustenance of members of such communities for the entire twelve months of the year.

The unemployment is caused among the tribals owing to growth of education. Those who have read even up to middle class want a government job and do not want to work in their field or to adopt their traditional craft. This has led to the situation of unemployment.

Urbanisation is another cause responsible for unemployment in tribal India. Industrialisation is yet another factor. These two have great bearing in causing unemployment in tribal India. L.P. Vidyarthi, Surjeet Sinha, Sachindra Narayan etc. have highlighted it in their studies.

Migration has also led to unemployment. Tribals migrate in search of a job and in many cases they do not get it leading to unemployment and economic frustration among the tribals.

Sachindra Narayan has discussed this in his article on Migration in Tribal Bihar (1982).

Unemployment is also the cost of development. The tribals were satisfied with their traditional occupation but the development plans made them ambitious causing unemployment among them. Culture contact is yet another contributory factor in causing unemployment in tribal India.

The unemployeds are of two kinds i. e. seasonal and permanent. The seasonal unemployed tribals migrate to states like Punjab, West Bengal, Jammu & Kashmir, Himachal Pradesh, Assam etc. To solve this kind of unemployment problem, programmes like NREP, MNP, IRDP etc. are being run by the government. But another interesting feature of unemployment in tribal India is also of underemployment. The tribals in employment generally feel that they are underemployed. Another dimension of the unemployment in tribal India is that in spite of reservation for tribals in government jobs there is unemployment in tribal India. This may be because of communication gap between private and public sector and tribals. The vacancies occurring in private and public sectors are not within the easy reach of poor tribals so they do not know and remain unemployed. Generally Employment Exchange offices are located in such a place where the poor tribals seldom reach.

Increasing rate of literacy and spread of education has also accelerated the problem of unemployment. The other factor adding to the problem of the unemployment is the tribals' attachment with the forest dwelling, their environment and ecology. The Sauria Paharias of Bihar were provided employment in theplains of Sahebganj but they refused it simply because they live on the top of the hills and do not like to come on the plains. Similarly Birhors of Bihar were also given employment but they refused owing to preference for own ecology and environment.

According to 1981 census the total workers in tribal India and Bihar are as follows ;

1981 Census	India Scheduled Tribe Total Worker	Non-worker
P	39.59	60.42
M	53.67	46.33
F	24.47	75.53
	Bihar	
P	45.92	54.08
M	57.03	42.97
F	34.74	65.26

In Chotanagpur, where there is only main kharif rice crop and another cash-crop during the rainy season, some intensity of employment cannot be expected as it is in the case of rest of Bihar. Evidences both direct as well as indirect suggest that employment for wages does not exceed 150 days in a year in Chotanagpur. Three alternatives are opened to them to fill up the gap : (a) self-employment in the village or nearby, (b) come to towns or temporarily migrate to towns in Chotanagpur during the slack season for employment on casual basis and (c) permanent or seasonal migration to distant places in Bihar and outside.

It is desirable to solve this problem that Employment Exchanges be located within the reach of the poor tribals. A list of technical graduates, postgraduates etc. be prepared at the district level and employment should be given strictly on the basis of this list. Programmes and policies should be formulated to encourage the self-employment. The traditional art and craft as well as occupation be revived under economic package programmes of the development. Further employment potentialities, should be created suiting to ecological and cultural needs of the tribals.

Tribal Agricultural Labourers

A tribal agricultural labour is he who works in another person's land for wages in cash, kind or share. Such a person has no risk in cultivation but merely works in another person's land for wages. An agricultural labourer has no right of lease or contact on land on which he works. The agricultural labourers is a subject matter of discussion among the anthropologists mainly because of prevalent 'money system' in major part of the tribal India. Under 'barter system' labour was also a subject of exchange and hence was not considered as one of the problems of the people of the tribal India.

As per the 1981 census the total population of the tribal agricultural labourers in India and in Bihares are as follows :

India

	Population	Male	Female
Total	7,174,898	3,846,309	3,328,589
Rural	6,966,583	3,723,425	3,243,158
Urban	2,08,315	1,22,884	85,431

Bihar

	Population	Male	Female
Total	5,810,867	2,915,492	2,895,375
Rural	5,447,750	2,725,758	2,722,992
Urban	3,62,117	1,89,734	1,72,383

Tribal Agricultural labour is primary problem of settled cultivators and also of primitive tribes. Most of the tribes who formerly were the land owners have turned agricultural labours owing to the land alienation and continuous exploitation. The total number of agricultural labourers has grown over the years. Some of the agricultural labourers have also become bonded labourers like Gond of Rohtas and Korwa of Palamau. Earlier there was no group of people in tribal India known as 'agricultural labourer'. There was mutual exchange of labour or the Dhumkuria (the youth dormitory) was extending support but now owing to increasing economic hardship it has become 'labourer' role. The economic role of agricultural labourers is just to support their economy and even with this they are unable to have two square meals. The specialisation of the economic role of agricultural labourers has given them an opportunity to migrate temporarily or permanently in the fields of Punjab, West Bengal, Assam, Kashmir etc.

To solve the problem of the agricultural labourers we have

to design special economic package projects. It needs special component plan to solve the problem of agricultural labourers. The NREP programme covers only those tribals who are coming in the fringe of the programmes. But the primitive and food gathering and hunting tribes are not being covered by the NREP programme. To solve this problem it is neccssary that the Forest and other allied departments falling within the tribal dwellings should employ only local tribals on daily wages. This cannot be solved in isolation. It needs a package of economic developmental inputs to solve the problems of agricultural labourer such as home based industry, triple farming, cash crop cultivation as well as health inputs.

Special problems of hunting and food gathering and other minor tribes

In development planning for any broad target group or area the socio-economic levels of different sub-groups and underdeveloped areas need attention. In the scheduled tribes of India, different groups are at different level of development. Similarly, of the 4.76 lakh sq. km. of tribal sub-plan area, some areas are totally undeveloped.

The question of tackling the problems of the more backward tribal communities has received the attention of various commissions and study teams. As has been alluded to, the Scheduled Areas and Scheduled Tribes Commission (1961) usually known as the Dhebar Commission observed amongst them four different layers. At the base, they identified a class of tribals in an extremely underdeveloped stage. Since this lowest layer needs the utmost consideration, they recommend that (a) it should be made the special concern of the state Governments and (b) the chief executive officers concerned with the task of implementing policies for its protection and development should be made specially responsible. Therefore, the study Team on Tribals Development Programmes (1969) (Shilu Ao Team) discerned, marked imbalance in the development among the tribal communities, a large number of tribal communities continuing to be extremely backward, some of them still in the primitive food gathering stage. They reiterated the view of the Dhebar Commission that the 'lowest layer' needed the uttermost consideration and should be made the special concern of the state Governments. The study team included in its report a list of backward tribal communities considered so by the Dhebar Commission, the Commissioner for scheduled castes and scheduled Tribes and the Team itself. However, the study Team regarded the classification as tentative calling for additions and alterations. They suggested that state Governments and administrations of Union Territories should make an objective study of the extent to which each of the tribal communities living in their respective areas had been fixed from the tribal development programme and select on the the basis of such a study the really backward communities needing special attention. Further, that separate schemes for imparting education and economic uplift should be formulated and treated as central schemes, including special provision in the plan for the purpose.

At the time of review of tribal development programmes on the eve of the Fifth Plan, it was recognised that special programmes for the extremely backward tribal groups, known as primitive groups, should be taken up on the basis of proper identification on the lines suggested by the Shilu Ao Team. It was also envisaged that the programmes would be financed wholly by the Ministry of Home Affairs.

As a preliminary step, a workshop on primitive tribal communities was held in the Ministry of Home Affairs in January 1975. Later the subject was discussed at the conference of Tribal Commissioners and state Chief Ministers held in October 1976. Detailed guidelines were issued for identification of primitive tribal groups.

In the guidelines issued by the Planning Commission on the preparation of First Tribal sub-plans, it was specifically indicated that (a) special attention should be given to the areas and the groups facing special problems including primitive tribal groups in backward pockets, shifting cultivators and tribals, affected by major projects (b) for the purpose, these communities and groups should be identified adopting well-defined criteria (c) the tribal sub-plan must attempt in broad terms answer for the main issues facing the tribal communities in these areas and the problems of special groups (d) special assistance be provided for such groups or communities against a basic policy frame which would vary from the general approach in the sectoral programmes unfettered by the existing formal, procedural or legal frame. The final course could be defined only after fully examining the impact of all the factors.

In the identification of primitive groups, states have generally followed three norms : (1) pre-agriculture level of technology (ii) low level of literacy and (iii) a stagnant or diminishing population. On the basis of these criteria 52 communities have been identified as primitive till the end of this year. A list of such communities, also indicating such groups which the Dhebar commission and the Shilu Ao Team also considered as primitive is as follows :

Primitive tribes (popularly known as hunter, food gatherer and food collector, nomadic etc.)

State	*Tribes*
Andhra Pradesh	1. Kolan
	2. Chenchers
	3. Kondu Reddi
Bihar	1. Birhor
	2. Mal Paharia
	3. Asurs
	4. Brijias
	5. Parhaiyas
	6. Korwas
	7. Hill Kharia
	8. Savar
	9. Sauria Paharia
Gujarat	1. Kathodi
	2. Kotwalia
Karnataka	1. Jammu Kursuba
	2. Koraga
Kerala	1. Kurumbas
	2. Chdauai Kayan
Madhya Pradesh	1. Abuyhamarias

	2. Baigas
	3. Bharias
	4. Hill Korbas
	5. Saharias
Maharashtra	1. Katkaria
	2. Kolam
	3. Maria Gond
Orissa	1. Bondo
	2. Soura
	3. Kharias
	4. Mankidias
	5. Katia Kondh
	6. Paudi Bhuyans
	7. Juang
	8. Linjia Sauras
	9. Bongaria Kondh
Rajasthan	1. Saharias
Tamil Nadu	1. Kotas
	2. Paniyans
	3. Todas
	4. Kattu Naickens
	5. Irulas
	6. Kurumbas
Tripura	1. Reangs
Uttar Pradesh	1. Rajis
West Bengal	1. Birhor
	2. Toto
	3. Lodha
Andaman and Nicobar Islands	1. Great Andamanese
	2. Onges
	3. Jarwas
	4. Sentinelese
	5. Shom Pens

The programme has been financed entirely by the Central Government out of the Special Central Assistance. The amounts released to the states from year to year have been :

Year	Rs. (in lakhs)
1975-76	31.00
1976-77	65.00
1977-78	77.00
1978-79	158.00
1979-80	157.00

(Provision for 1978-83 for the programmes is Rs. 10 crores)

A scrutiny of the project reports prepared for the development of the primitive tribes reveals that much improvement is needed to be effected in bringing about a clear focus of the salient problem of the groups and thus to solve their problem it may be recommended that :

(i) High priority should be given to the programme of primitive groups in the current plan.

(ii) Identification of primitive tribal groups in accordance with the guidelines already issued should be expedited.

(iii) There should be unique programme for each group.

(iv) The programmes must specially take into consideration the eco-system.

(v) The first phase of development should aim at conservation and reorganisation of the traditional skills of the groups.

(vi) The second phase should spell out the development programme.

Separate organisational structure should be created, with sensitive project officers at the executive head charged with the specific responsibility of properly handling and developing these communities. It is the human touch of the individual that will determine the quality of the programme and the future of the community. Some sanctions should be applied on those states which don't create appropriate administrative apparatus or follow the right personnel policies. Voluntary organisations could also be entrusted the task. Special regulations might be promulgated to protect the command over resources of the groups.

4

PROBLEM OF CULTURAL CONTACT

The tribals of India are rich in their cultural heritage and ecology. They are at various levels of cultural and economic development. They are scattered throughout the country. With the independence of the country some protective measures were taken for safeguarding their interests. Professor Verrier Elwin in his book 'A Philosophy for NEFA' puts forth the principles of (a) Isolation (b) Assimilation and (c) Integration which later on served the guideline in formulating the policies for the tribal development.

Isolation

In the past the tribals were looked down upon on the one hand, as 'simple creatures of the earth' and praised for their simplicity and honesty on the other. But in modern India in spired by lofty ideals of human dignity, equality and social justice, the government took keen interest in the problems of the aboriginals who were far removed from the main currents of civilization. The problem of the aboriginals development posed many intricate problems which resulted in different theories. Among the important theories put forward by thinkers, one is the policy of isolation. The policy of isolation is commonly attributed to the influence of anthropologists. They are invariably accused of wanting to keep the tribals in the zoos or museums for their own purposes. It is alleged that during discussion on the 'excluded areas' in February, 1963, the anthropologists wanted to keep the tribals in a perpetual 'state of barbarism' in order to add to their 'blessed stock of scientific knowledge'. It was feared by the anthropologists and their fear proved to be justified in Madhya Pradesh and Bihar (The Study of a tribe—A study in tribal dynamics 1960, D.N. Majumdar) the where contacts with the people from the outside world had a debasing influence leading to economic exploitation and cultural degeneration.

Dr. Verrier Elwin argues that nothing positive was being done for their welfare, national workers were not admitted into their hills, but merchants, money lenders, landlord missionaries were destroying their art and dances, their weaving and their whole culture.

The tribals coming into contact with the non-tribals tried to imitate their life style, world view, ethos and also the economy. Their such contact with the non-tribals consequently also brought change in their occupation pattern. Some of the tribes like Mahli of Chotanagpur lost their traditional occupation. The cultural contact has also brought technological change in their traditional life. Introduction of intermediary technological inputs and heavy engineering have greatly changed their socio-cultural-economic life. L.P. Vidyarthi has amply emphasised in his study the Impact of HEC on the tribals of Ranchi. There he has shown that in what way and to what extent the HEC has changed the poor tribals. Such change occurred because the non-tribals in good number started living in and around HEC and the presence of such non-tribals gradually influenced them in all respect. To day we hardly find tribals in and around HEC attached to their tribal ethos. The cultural contact also led to change in their own traditional political system. In one of my studies (1979) I have amply demonstrated how the traditional tribal system is being replaced by the statutory panchayat system. This has also brought change in their traditional education system. This I have also shown in one of my studies (1978) that how Dhumkuria got weakened in tribal India and is on the verge of extinction among the tribals. However, the modern education system is also not reacting properly in tribal India. The impact of cultural contact has also resulted in gradual loss of folktales and folksongs in tribal India. The cultural contact has also introduced urbanization and industrialisation in tribal India.

Urbanisation

Urbanisation is a process of social and cultural change in which the tribal and the rural India is gradually changing towards urban centres. This is because of the planned change induced by the five year plans of the country. Urbanisation in tribal India is a social dimension caused by the problems of cultural contacts with the tribals who were living in remote areas surrounded by the forest or at the top of the hills. But after the independence of the country, constitutionally it was desired that the tribals of the country should also be brought into the mainstream of the country. Conveniently various developmental measures were taken for the upliftment of tribal India. Such measures caused more problems to the tribals than solving their problems and that is why we are facing more the problem of urbanisation. But it does not mean that the urbanisation was not at all required in tribal India. But fact is that it was required with some planning and anthropological insight and strategies. However, the overall impact of the urbanisation is visible. Urbanisation has changed the dwelling pattern of the tribals. In one of my studies (1986), I have mentioned that the lands which were being used for agriculture purposes are now used for residential purposes. The houses of Santhals, Oraons, Mundas etc in tribal India were no constructed systematically and scientifically but now if one goes to Karmtoli or Kantatoli or Hinoo locality of Ranchi one is amused to see the housing pattern. It is just contrary to their traditional dwelling pattern.

The urbanisation has also caused change in their life style. Earlier, after attending natural call in the field, they were washing their hands in the nearby pond which is also used by and for animals and other such purposes. Thereafter either they go to forest or to farm to continue their day. But now owing to urbanisation they use bath room, wash basin and have developed the concept of 'clean water', 'drinking water' 'safe water', 'filtered water' etc. Instead of going to forest and to farm they go to office, workshop, factory etc.

Change in the lifestyle has also brought change in their food habits and dress. In a city like Patna, the tribals brick kiln labourers wear pants and shirts and even when they return to their respective villages, they continue to wear it because they can't afford to buy other clothes to be worn in village. After sometime this becomes their habit and they do not like to wear traditional dresses.

The allied change has also occurred in their religious belief, world view ethos etc. The process of urbanisation has made them tolerant towards other religions. It has been mentioned elsewhere that the tribals in urban areas are no longer interested in maintaining their sarba. Living together has inculcated tolerance for other sects and they are extending ahelping hand to other followers of other sects even in the matter of construction of sacred places. Urbanisation has also greatly influenced their ecology. The employment pattern and occupational pattern in tribal India has also undergone change owing to urbanisation. Instead of traditional employment and occupational pattern they prefer to work in offices, factories, workshops, shops, etc. The traditional craftsmen like blacksmiths carpenters etc. are dwindling rather such population are working as peons, clerks etc, in Govt. and private offices, and factories. Most of them have even forgotten their traditional skills. To conclude we may say that urbanisation has a deterrent impact on the lifestyle, religious, political, social and economic life in tribal India.

Industrialisation

It is a notable coincidence that the central India tribal belt stranding across the states of West Bengal, Bihar, Orissa, Madhya Pradesh, Andhra Pradesh has been burgeoning into a zone of intense industrial and mining activities in the recent decades. The Durgapur, Bokaro, Jamshedpur, Rourkela, Bhilai Steel Plants, the Ranchi Heavy Engineering Complex, a host of ancillary industries, a chain of mining complexes have also made appearance in the tribal belt. A hoary agroforest traditional culture has been confronted with a modern sophisticated industrial culture. The abrupt juxtaposition has produced deleterious results for the tribals. There has been large-scale alienation of tribal land for the public and private enterprises etc. Having lost the basic resource, the tribals have not been able to secure alternative sources of livelihood. The first generation has found it nearly impossible to imbibe the skills and culture of the industrial age. It would appear that the shock impulses generated on account of the imposition of the modern industry have been beyond the absorption capacity of the tribal communities. In fact, for the first generation, it has been an unmitigated disaster, in as much as it has meant nearly wholesale destruction. The question whether industrialisation planned for the tribal areas should not contend with the human sacrifice involved, acquires significance. Should not the interests of tribal men and women be safeguarded while planning therefor ?

It is crystal clear, however, that we cannot keep in check the advancing tide of industrialisation. Nevertheless, we can soften the rigours of the new alien climate. The tribals can be prepared beforehand to participate in industrialisation or in the alternative to make gainful living notwithstanding the establishment of the new industry. But no step should be taken which is clearly foreseen to ensure the destitution of masses of innocent men and women.

The Ministry of Home Affairs have appointed a committee consisting of administrators, academics and representatives of the Ministeries of Industrial Development and Education, to advise on the future lines of development in the central India belt particularly in and around industrial complexes with aview to minimising adverse effects and involvement of tribals in the process of industrialisation. We have no doubt that the Government would consider the recommendations of the committee carefully and initiate appropriate measures to esure the tribal interests promptly.

Establishment of all major and medium industries is normally preceded by feasibility studies, project reports etc. which focus attention mostly on technical input output factors. We suggest that no project report should be deemed complete without inclusion therein of consideration of future of the local communities based on study of all related aspects like the present socio-economic status, cultural profile and the anthropology of the perspective developments, by interdisciplinary teams composed of plant technologists etc. The project report should spell out (a) positive and negative repercussions flowing from the establishment of the industry on the local communities (b) steps reqired to be taken for their active involvement in the industry, (c) steps for continuation of traditional avocations, culture etc. of those members who stay out. In more concrete terms, land should be acquired or purchased from tribals only when strictly necessary rather than cash compensation which disappears within no time, allotment of suitable land in exchange should be the general rule. Skills should be imparted in advance to enable availability of the industrial opportunities in the new establishment, if not the first generation, some individuals belonging to the second generation might absorb the skills. The ability to face the harsh forces of the modern industrial age has to be built up in tribals through constant education. Adequate financial provision should be made for all these measures.

We understand that the Government of India had a little while ago, taken decision that the development of zones of influence of industrial and mining complexes should be prepared as a part of the project report. The idea being that investment in these areas should develop a region rather than a small localised industrial or mining complex. We are not aware of the progress in the matter. We feel that such planning exercises would be useful not only for prospective projects but also in respect of the existing industrial and mining ones. Tribal areas should become productive hinter lands. The tribal family displaced from home and hearth should be given viable rehabilitation.

The working group of Tribal Development (1978-83) had recommended that the bureau of public enterprises should take up leadership role at the national level for the location of industries in tribal areas and should be concerned with the public sector project which form the buck. The steps taken are not yet known. Since sudden intensive economic activities in the industrial regions has detrimental effect on the economy and anthropology of scheduled tribes there should be clear perception about activity to be taken up. Suitable regulation should be framed so that constitution at the highest level becomes a prerequisite to setting up big industries in tribal areas. It has appeared that licensing committees have been set up in the concerned ministries to scrutinise in various aspects before issuing the licences. To ensure that the scrutiny does not overlook the tribal angle, it would be advantageous to place a representative of the Home Ministry on these Committces. In the states also a representative or representatives of the Department of Tribal Development might be associated with similar committees or bodies.

Impact

The expectation that the industrialisation of tribal areas would help in improving the economic condition of the tribal communities has proved to be largely illusory. Major industrial projects like the mammoth level steel plants located in tribal territory far from generating employment for the tribals have operated to their detriment by uprooting them from their hearths and offering them no satisfactory alternative to the traditional methods by which they eked out a living in their old geographical and technological environment. The attitude of the projects even in the public sector has been that their responsibility to the tribals ended with the payment of compensation for the land acquired from them. A meagre cost compensation is soon frittered away on drink and users products and destitution is the price the poor tribal has to pay for the establishment of industries in the areas inhabited by them.

The major power and irrigation projects, such as the Maithon, Konar and Parchet in Bihar, the Mandira, Mackkund and Hirakund in Orissa, West Bengal, Madhya Pradesh and Bihar respectively are among the many undertakings that have resulted in a substantial displacement of the tribal people. This was inevitable but what is needed is a social approach to a problem of deep moral significance.

As an example of general failure in tackling the problem of rehabilitation of displaced tribals, Dhebar Commission reveals that out of 14,561 tribal families of Bihar, West Bengal and Orissa displaced from 62,494 acres, only 3479 were allotted alternative land. The situation is far from happy for the following reasons :

(a) Very few of them have taken advantage of the agricultural facilities offered in the reclamation camps. The attraction of easy money and industrial employment has been too strong, especially for the younger generation.

(b) The alternative land offered by the authorities for cultivation is not irrigable and cannot offer adequate return to maintain the families on it.

(c) The cash compensation that is given is seldom utilized for productive purposes. It is almost invariably used on daily living expenses until alternative employment is found.

L. P. Vidyarthi reinforces the proof of the failure to rehabilitate the displaced tribals by providing an example from H.E.C. Ltd, Ranchi. The undertaking is situated in the middle of Chotanagpur, a predominantly tribal region. The position of employment of the local tribals as on January 1, 1972 was as follows :—

Category	Total employment	Total number of scheduled tribe employees
Category 1	1,230	24
" 2	779	16
" 3	10,748	1,154
" 4	5,336	1,618
Total	18,093	2,812

Further no space is provided to the tribals in the newly constructed township on the site of the project. They are left to construct and inhabit dirty slums on the outskirts or on the vacant lands in the township itself. These slums are without any civic amenities like tap water, garbage disposal, drainage etc.

Another table, a more comprehensive one, may be cited in support of the fact that very little is done to rehabilitate the displaced tribals. The table given below provides an idea of the quantum of relief provided in terms of rehabilitation to the displaced tribals as a result of establishment of major projects in the tribal area.

The gravity of the situation may be gauged from the fact that the above table does not include data from Bihar and Orissa, inclusion of which shall only add to the seriousness of the charge of callousness and negligence on the responsible bureaucrats who soundly complain that this problem is presen ted in inflated form by the social workers and political agitators to malign the administration.

Years	No. of displaced families.	Total average land of displaced persons.	No. of rehabilitated families.	Acreage of total allocated land.
1968-69+	817	5,887	309	—
1969-70+	2,399	20,095	1,412	2,036
1970-71+	40	103	18	28
1971-72++	4,561	21,199	1,587	3,959
1972-73++	2,310	10,550	590	305

+Data pertaining to Kerala, Gujarat, Madhya Pradesh, Maharashtra, Rajasthan, Tamil Nadu, West Bengal and Himachal Pradesh only.

++Data pertaining to Maharashtra, Manipur, West Bengal and Rajasthan only.

Industrialization has disturbed the peace of the tribal India. They are yet to adopt the factory or office life hence cultural adjustment problem is there. Tribals are accustomed to seasonal or agricultural labour but owing to industrialisation they have to work round the year. Industrialisation has broken the joint family system prevalent in tribal India. Now they are having nuclear family. Traditional authority of the elders in the family has been considerably weakened. Traditional norms and practices are being flouted by the industrialised tribals. Tribals are generally advancing towards integration with the general mass of people but at the same time they are losing rapidly their traditional social cultural characteristics. In their traditional agrarian economy the family was functioning more or less as a unit of labour. In the factories however it is the individual who is wanted since not much data are available about the problems of psychological and socio-cultural adjustment it is difficult to gauge the impact of industrialisation from this particular angle. But one thing is fairly clear from the membership of a close society he is being induced to accommodate himself is a universal pattern of cosmopolitan society without education, equipment and resources. There is a crisis of identity. Industrialisation has bred new drinking habits, prostitution, feud, unionism, unemployment, migration and loss of agricultural land in tribal India.

Depopulation

Depopulation is a term widely used by physical anthropologists. However, the term has an applied value in anthropology. Depopulation denotes dwindlement of the population. There are some tribes in tribal India whose population are gradually dwindling viz. Shampen, Onge Yanadi, Sauria Paharia etc. In one of my studies on the dwindling nature of the tribe it has been found that the Sauria Paharia are actually dwindling. According to my study 'The Sauria Paharia—A Development Perspective (10-24,1981)" the number of occupied residential houses of Karam Village is 22. Total population of the village is 88, male 24, female 27 with male child 22 and female child is 15. The second village is Chota Pachrukhi and the number of residential houses is 15. Total population of village is 62—17 are male with same number of female. 14 are male child and the similar number is of female child. Third village is Bara Pachrukhi consisting of 17 houses. With the population of 76, in which male are 19, female are 28 and male child are 17 and female child are 12. The fourth village is Ladouni. The number of houses is 18. The total population is 68—male 23, female 29 with 8 male child and equal number of female child.

The fifth village is Pachgarh. There is no population in the village. The Paharia living in this village have migrated to another village.

The following table give detailed break up of population at subdivision, Block and village levels.

TABLE 1
Urban Population 1971

No. of houses	Total population			Scheduled tribe		Literate and educated rerson	
	P	M	F	M	F	M	F
6,207	35,640	19,389	16,259	286	170	12,451	6,002

TABLE 2
Rural Population 1971 (Borio Block)

No. of houses	Total population			Scheduled tribes		Literate and educated persons	
	P	M	F	M	F	M	F
18,389	93,282	46,534	46,748	30,992	33,026	6,043	1,272

TABLE 3
Age and Sexwise Distribution of total population of five villages, 1980

Age groups	Male	% of population	Female	% of population
0-4	33	22.9	19	12.9
5-9	18	12.5	19	12.9
10-14	10	6.9	11	7.5
15-19	8	5.5	9	6.1
20-24	10	6.9	21	14.3
25-29	16	11.1	14	9.5
30-34	13	9.0	17	11.6
35-39	14	9.8	19	12.9
40-44	14	9.8	10	6.8
45-49	5	3.5	7	4.8
50-54	3	2.1	1	0.7
Total	144	100.00	147	100.00

TABLE 4

Age and Sexwise Distribution of Population—1980 of Karam Pahar

Agc group	Male	Female
0-4	12	5
5-9	5	8
10-14	5	2
15-19	2	3
20-24	4	6
25-29	4	3
30-34	4	4
35-39	5	3
40-44	6	2
45-49	1	2
50 +	1	1
85—over	—	—
Total	49	39

Total population=49+39=88

TABLE 5

Age and Sexwise Distribution of Total Population of Chotta Pachrukhi

Age group	Male	Female
0-4	7	7
5-9	6	3
10-14	1	4
15-19	2	2
20-24	2	8
25-29	4	0
30-34	1	1
35-39	1	4
40-44	3	1
45-49	2	1
50 +	2	—
Total	31	31

Total population=31+31=62.

TABLE 6

Age and Sexwise Distribution of Population of Bara Pachrukhi

Age groups	Male	Female
0-4	10	5
5-9	5	4
10-14	2	3
15-19	1	2
20-24	1	3
25-29	4	5
30-34	4	7
35-39	3	6
40-44	3	3
45-49	1	2
50 +	0	0
Total	36	40

Total Population=36+40=76

TABLE 7

Population—1971

No. of houses—18	P	M	F	SC Tribes M	F
	70	32	38	32	31

Population—1980
No. of houses—18

P	M	F
68	31	37

TABLE 8

Population 1980

Age and Sexwise distribution of population of Ladauni

Age groups	Male	Female
0-4	4	2
5-9	2	4

10-14	2	2
15-19	3	2
20-24	3	4
25-29	4	6
30-34	4	5
35-39	5	6
40-44	2	2
45-49	1	2
50 +	0	0
Total	37	31

Total Population=37+31=68

TABLE 9

Years	Population
1872	68,335
1891	1,11,592
1901	47,006
1921	62,734
1931	55,600
1941	59,891
1951	58,654
1961	53,576
1971	55,606

In the preceding, Tables (from 1-9) the total population of the Paharia at district, subdivision, block and village levels has been given. The Table population of the Paharias at district level shows fluctuation at decinial variation but such figures are not available for those villages as have been undertaken for the present study. However, a detailed break up of age wise population has been also done to ascertain the reasons of such fluctuation but unfortunately in the abcence of decinial variation of the population of the villages it becomes difficult to assign any reason for such fluctuation.

If the population of Ladauni villages of 1971 given at Table 7 is taken into account it reveals that the total population of the village has decreased from 70 to 68 during 10 years period. It indicates that the growth of population in this village is –2.8%. If it is considered representative population it becomes an indicator of declining population.

It is evident from the total population of the Sauria Paharia that there is a fluctuation in the decinial population of this tribe. It is difficult to indicate any factor responsible for such fluctuation in the absence of such field data. The Sauria Paharia live on hill tops. The indifference of these people to government officials also becomes a hinderance for enumerator to visit them. The Paharias are known as criminal tribe in police vocabulary. Villages of the Sauria Paharia are inaccessible. It is just possible that under the circumstances the census enumerators might not have visited the villages located on top of the hills and an estimated population might have been projected in the census report. A long term project carried out on the Sauria Paharia may reveal the real responsible factors. However, on the basis of the Table no. 7 it is evident that the growth rate of the population of the village Ladouni is —2.8 during 1971-80. If it is taken as an indicator of the growth rate of the population of the Sauria Paharia then it can be said as a declining population. The following Table gives the detail of percentage decadal variation of population of the Santhal Pargana district.

TABLE 10

Census year	1901-11	1911-21	1921-31	1931-41	1941-51	1951-61	1961-71
% of the population growth in Santhal Pargana Dist.	+4.04	—4.46	+14.30	+8.99	+3.92	+15.21	+19.13

The above Table does not show any declining trend in the population but a decrease in the scheduled tribe population of Santhal Pargna i.e. rather peculiar, because the population of the district is largely tribal in comparison. However, when the tribewise statistics are examined for 1941 and 1961 it becomes apparent that none of the tribes, except the Sauria Paharia has actually decreased in numbers. As a matter of fact the over all increase of the tribal population from 1941 census has been of the order of 10 per cent. A look at the total population of the Sauria Paharia suggests that the Sauria Paharia are the only scheduled tribe whose population has consistently been falling from 1931, though the rate of decrease has been slow i.e. 2.1 per cent in 1931-41 and 5.1 per cent in 1941-61.

TABLE 11

Population of Sauria Paharia—1941 and 1961 with variations.
Total Population :—

1941	58,654
1961	55,606
Variation	—3,048
Percentage Variation	—5.2

It suggests that the total population of the Sauria Paharia presented a decreasing trend and thus the population of Ladauni which has percentage variation of (minus) 2.8 during 71-80 can be considered a representative population of the Sauria Paharia.

The following table gives the total population of India and Bihar at one place and also the age and sex distribution of the population. The subsequent table gives the age and sex wise distribution of the total population of the five studied villages of Borio Block of Rajmahal subdivision during 1980 (Field Data).

TABLE 12
(Population 000)

Age group	India Total	1971 Male	Femal	Total	Bihar Male	Femal
0-14	23,02,54	11,88,70	1,13,84	2,39,94	1,25,05	11,48,9
15-19	4,44,47	2,52,11	2'22,36	4490	2373	2117
20-24	43082	21563	21520	4301	2029	2272
25-29	40799	20327	20473	4155	2029	2126
30-39	69057	35540	33517	7333	3649	3684
40-49	51155	27515	23640	5424	2839	2585
50-59	33345	17985	15361	3338	1765	1562
60 and above	32693	16871	15822	3324	1656	1668
known	116	56	60	5	2	3
Total	547950	283937	264013	56353	28847	27506

TABLE-13

Age and sexwise distribution of total population of the five studied villages of Borio Block of Sahebganj subdivsion (now district) of 1980 (Field data)

Age group	Male	Female	Total
0-4	33	19	52
5-9	18	19	37
10-14	10	11	21
15-19	8	9	17
20-24	10	21	31
25-29	16	14	30
30-34	13	17	30
35-39	14	19	33
40-44	14	10	24
45-49	5	7	12
50-54	3	1	4
Total	144	147	291

Child Women ratio

1. $\frac{0\text{-}4c}{15\text{-}44W} \times 1000 = 578$

2. $\frac{0\text{-}4c}{15\text{-}49W} \times 1000 = 536$

3. $\frac{5\text{-}9c}{20\text{-}49W} \times 1000 = 420$

4. $\frac{5\text{-}9c}{20\text{-}54W} \times 1000 = 416$

India : Child Women ratio during 1961—68 is 675

Bihar : Child Women ratio : 1877

India : Child Women ratio : 1897

If the Child women ratio is calculated of G.R.F. Principles, the women ratio between 0—4 child it comes to 578 and 536 and between 5-9 it comes to 420 and 416. If the 578 and 536 considered as the population of four years ago from the date of data collection it suggest the population of Sauria Paharia as a declining population according to G.R.F. .

The child-women ratio of India is :

$$\frac{C0\text{-}14}{W\text{-}15\text{-}49} = \frac{23,254}{12388} \times 1000 = 1897$$

Child women ratio of Bihar is :

$$\frac{C0\text{-}14}{W\text{-}15\text{-}49} = \frac{23994}{1,27,84} \times 1000 = 1877$$

Child women ratio of Sauria Paharia of Santhal Pargana is :

$$\frac{C0\text{-}14}{W\text{-}15\text{-}49} = \frac{22873}{2,66,40} \times 1000 = 882$$

Child women ratio of selected villages is—578. This also suggests that the C. W. ratio of Sauria Paharia is quite low in comparison to total population of India and Bihar and of Sauria Paharia of Santhal Pargana and therefore it is a declining population.

Regionalism

Regionalism may be viewed in the context of process of change going on in India in general and in tribal India in particular from persisting traditionalism to modernization and in terms of in varying pole in different socio-cultural, economic and political spheres.

Features of Regionalism

1. Regionalism, usually based on language and economic disparities and regional sectarian politics is strong. Its importance lies in the fact that the people seem to identify themselves more easily in terms of district sub-cultural groups belonging to different regions whose interest clash, than as Indians belonging to a political entity known as India.

2. Power structure in the villages is changing economic and political power in the welfare of the elite tribals, neorich tribals and educated tribals.

3. There is more stress on localman theory. A much

greater number of regional political leaders and spokesmen with narrow vision are emerging and there is a sharp decline in the number and quality of leaders who are truly national and have an outlook free from regional moorings and loyalties.

4. The increasing conflicts between the centre and states.

5. Decline in centre's authority and greater assertion of states

6. Weakening of the national sentiment.

As a result of these features certain disintegrating forces seem to be growing stronger. The ones emanating from regionalism are :—

1. Sectarian pulls by regional political parties.

2. Regional bias of the state units of the all India political parties.

3. Inter regional disparities and tensions over linguistic economic and political parties.

4. Regional ethnocentricism.

5. Revivalist movements for preserving the culture and safeguarding the 'state right'.

6. Increase in provincialism linguism, and lack of proper appreciation by a regional groups of the way of life, customs and cultural attainment of minority groups within their region and of major groups in other regions.

7. Increase in militant sub-nationalism and infranationalism subsequently expressed through socio-cultural and separation movement.

Tribal Ethos and Integration

The tribal population in India, as elsewhere, has lived in a comparative isolation and is somewhat apart from the mainstream of society. Partly because of their isolation and partly because of their limited world view characterised by lack of historical depth and overall tradition orientation, they are integrated in terms of certain themes rooted in the past. These integrative themes and a special cultural force has given them a separate cultural identity and they often possess latent or manifest value attitude and motivational system which are remarkably different from those of other people. This distinctive rthos relises for them a series of problems of social, economic and general cultural adjustment. The tribal population are varied in terms of their ethnic, linguistic, economic and social characteristics.

The Naga situation is well known and the series of movements launched by them to stage a break from the vast of the Indian Nation amptly reflects the gravity of the situation in the north-east India. While in the rest of the country the Nagas are considered to be the simplest people. Among the Nagas themselves there is no primitive complex which is dominant self image. Their self image as rightly put by Roy Burman transverses across a primitive nation continuum. Roy Burman locates a type of movement termed 'infra-nationalism' which is found among the tribes of north-eastern India. He refers to infranationalism as a phase of expansion. Infra-nationalism overtakes a primitive community living in isolation and unacquainted with or uncommitted to national symbols and national goals. Infra-nationalism in its process of development extends clan loyalties to tribal loyalties and the tribal loyalties to intertribal loyalties. In this search for ethnic and regional solidarity the tribals develop regional-linguistic affinity and a common cultural and historical identity to boost their political aspirations. It is interesting to note as to how the Naga divided into numerous linguistic and factional groups are in search of establishing Nagamese as their common LINGUA FRANCA and the greater Nagaland as their national state.

Several points of view have been proposed to explain the category of infra-nationalism prevalent in north-eastern tribal area. Some attribute the separate posture of a large section of Nagas and other tribes in the region to prompting by foreign missionaries and the colonial rulers on the eve of their departuie. There are some who think that the regionalism or separatism of the Nagas has been prompted by the 'educated middle class' in their self interest. They advance irrefutable evidence in support of their stand and suggest solutions of the Naga problem in their own respective ways. Recently it has been suggested that the ethnic aspirations of the communities concerned is the crucial factor in determining the course of events. This ethnic aspiration of the Nagas and other tribes is part of the current restlessness in all the hill areas of south-east Asia. According to this point of view the role of Christian missionaries of the educated middle class has been only incidentally associated with this restlessness of the hill communities which really is the outcome of historical development.

The tribal belt of middle India has been characterized by the Jharkhand movement launched for the formation of separate state of the tribals in middle India. The tribal communities in middle India have been in closer contact with the regional culture of Hinduism and, in many ways, have contributed to as well as been influenced by it. The major tribal communities of this region which witnessed several revitalization movements during the nineteenth century have been under the process of integration with the rest of the regional culture. However, owing to certain other regions of the country this could be characterized by the concept of non-nationalism and regionalism.

Economic and Psychological Frustration

The tribal area of middle India during the recent times has been further exposed to modern influences owing to the exploitation of mineral resources, establishment of mineral based industries, emergence of industrial, commercial and administrative centres etc. The pace of industrialisation and with it that of urbanization has been greatly accelerated in this belt and specially in Chotanagpur after India's independence. The number of towns related with (1) mining, (2) manufacturing, (3) communication and (4) power projects increased greatly. With this the urban population also increased rapidly and all these developments brought about considerable change in the life ways of the local people. A section of the local people had to face land alienation and a phase of social disruption. Our studies of culture change among the tribals of middle India lead us to infer that the net result of the uprooting of the tribals, in due course, is loss of traditional occupation, land, house, the traditional way of life, exhaustion of cash received by way of compensation, unemployment, keen and unfair competition with the immigrants in labour markets, high aspirations and great frusturation. In view of these current disruptive forces and changing aspirations certain sections of educated, urbanized, and politically conscious tribal communities have taken up the challenge of the time and have prepared themselves to give lead to their innocent tribal brethren in the new situation. The general climate in this country has also given them impetus to press the demand for a separate state of Jharkhand and agitate for maximum advantage for their respective groups which find expression in tribalism, regionalism, localism and sometimes in religious extremism. In the wake of modernizing and secularizing forces released in middle India, the tribal leaders have found themselves helpless to fight the battle at the ethnic or religious levels. Their frustrations have found expression in the organization of a leadership on ethnic level, in the unrest of the tribal students and the consolidation of the tribal elite under pan-Christian organizations and so on.

Solutions for Regionalism

Provisions in the Indian constitution were made with the lofty objects to bridge the present socio-economic distance between the tribals and the rest of the population. At the moment there is a rising political and cultural consciousness among them. They have begun to feel more deeply than even before that they are less educated, less economically advanced and in several instances also not regarded as equals by other section of the population. This state of affairs has to be corrected.

There should be contacts, frank exchange of view and flow of information and ideas between the leaders and laymen of the tribal areas, and those of the rest of the nation on multiple platforms.

Psychological

At the psychological level efforts should be made for the rational appreciation of the regional stereotypes, dogmatic beliefs, ideas and half truths ; inculcation of national symbols, collective image of India, common cultural symbols, common cultural norms, through deliberate propoganda by the mass media and voluntary agencies should be attempted in the tribal areas.

Economic

At the economic level, the balanced economic development of all sub-cultural regions should be emphasised to remove inter-regional economic jealousies, equality of opportunity in the economic sphere has also to be ensured. Moreover, scope should be given even for the fulfilment of the political aspirations of aggrieved regions in a way that does not jeopardise regional balance and national unity.

Socio-cultural

The socio-cultural solution lies in the realization of the need for developing infra and inter-regional understanding and mutual toleration for each other's languages and ways of life. The genius of Indian civilization to co-exist in unity in spite of disparity be given due consideration. However, they need not influence our political and economic interdependence at the national level.

Others

Along with these economic, cultural and psychological solutions the need for a strong centre is the first requisite in the absence of which regional issues are bound to dominate and regulate the national issues to a secondary position. The economic and political grievances of the different regions should be considered with justice and impartiality, a forced unity does not last long. The political system should be such that it comprehends as a composite index of nationalism and national interrelation. But it should be overpowering enough to dominate over the negative aspect of infranationalism and regionalism or subnationalism. As rightly stated by Romesh Thapar, "The future is dependent largely on the degree to which the centre can assert itself not as a 'mix' of contradictory regional involvement but as a supreme arbiter of the national 'interest'. The leaders of the scheduled areas have also to play their rightful roles in this regard in the name of 'patriotism'.

5

HISTORY OF TRIBAL ADMINISTRATION IN INDIA

Before Independence

The so-called aborigines have been even much before independence a subject of research. They have been printed in different colours by different people. Hence, the general masses in India have been holding and perpetuating somewhat confusing and amazing and sometimes fantastic myths about this section of the society. Their image of primitive, simple, cheerful and colourful people having exotic dances and music, Ghotul, Rorung and Dhumkuria is based on several myths. Behind these myths lie a bitter reality—heart breaking poverty, ignorance, disease and exploitation. It is heartening to note that a number of honest scholars and researchers refused to be swayed by more romanticism and have scrupulously portrayed the ugly reality as it is.

The British administrators of pre-independence India were probably the first people who tried to grapple seriously with the problem of administering the tribal areas and they had a vested interest in cultivating and perpetuating the above-mentioned myths about the tribal people of India. They did everything to ensure that the so-called aborigines, the scheduled tribes remain isolated from the rest of the Indian masses because the British imperialist had realised the potentiality of Indian tribes as explosive force in any national movement. The tribals were isolated and their places of habitation were declared as prohibited area. Thus the alien rulers and Christian missionaries were the only people who had access to the tribal areas in the initial stages.

The first serious attempt made by the British rulers in India, to deal with the local aborigines was in connection with the Paharias or Sauria Paharia of Rajmahal Hills. The implicit intention behind this beginning was to deal with 'turbulent' tribes only. Leaders of these tribes were granted Sanad and they were assigned the responsibility of reporting all outbreaks. Ghurye (1963) writes that those leaders living near the lines of communication were to be paid a fixed sum to protect the mail runners. The payment is described by the competent authorities as "a bribe pure and simple as in 'Musalman' days. At the foot of the hills, lands were granted to retired or disabled soldiers and thus a ring fence of military people was created round the surrounding Paharias. Slowly working through the corps that were raised, a court was appointed from the officers of the corps for purpose of administration of justice. Encouraged by its utility, the government was approached to withdraw the Rajmahal hill tract from jurisdiction of the ordinary courts. Thus in 1882 this tribal tract was withdrawn from the jurisdiction of the ordinary courts and the hereditary leaders of the tribe were called into a sessions courts which was to meet twice a year and try all offences. The Council came to be known as hill assembly and it had the power to inflict or pass even capital punishment.

Having achieved the objective of internal justice and peace through the creation of the hill Assembly, Cleveland, the clever administrator tried to solve another important problem—the problem of encroachment by the hated 'foreigners'. The land held by the Paharias was formed into government estate held by them direct from Government and free from rent. These measures induced those Paharia chiefs who had still held out to join in and accept the rule of the British, which for all practical purposes was their own rule. The whole tract thus unified and specially treated came to be known as 'Daman-e-Koli' (Ghurye, 1963). In this way the turbulent and problematic Paharias were pacified and the rules were made law as Regulation I of 1796. With the passage of time, the prestige of Hill Assembly dwindled and the Regulation I of 1796 was replaced by Regulation I of 1827.

At this stage some other tribal groups, groaning under the yoke of exploitation rebelled. In this context such uprisings as Ho mutiny of Singhbhum in 1831, Khond uprising of 1946 and famous Santhal rebellion of 1855 are worth mentioning The British Indian Government was also forced to send punitive expeditions to Assam, Nagaland and Jaintia hills between 1850 and 1890 and repeatedly to the Lushai hills, Naga hills and to the Abor during the last decade of 19th century and the first decade of 20th century. The underlying causes of these uprisings and disturbances were almost the same. The deep resentment and dissatisfication created as a result of exploitation by their technologically and culturally more advanced neighbours.

At this stage the idea that "distinct and special arrangements were necessary for isolated tribal regions gained" general acceptance. The finding of anthropological researches seemed to support it. The British Government finally decided on a policy segregating the tribes into special areas where their lives and interest could supposedly be adequately protected. Keeping this purpose in mind an Act was passed in 1874 to specify tribal areas into scheduled District. These areas were reconstituted under section 52A of the Government of India Act of 1919. This Act provided for the appointment of officers to administer civil and criminal justice, to supervise the settlement and collection of public revenues and all matters relating to rent and otherwise to conduct the administration within the scheduled districts. It also provided for the extensions by notification to the scheduled districts, laws in force in any part of British India with such special restrictions and modifications as were deemed fit. Thus wide powers of legislation by simple execution order were vested in the Executive with the freedom movement gaining momentum, there was increasing anxiety on the part of the British administration to isolate the tribes from the national mainstream. The Indian statutory commission (Simon Commission) suggested that on financial and constitutional grounds the responsibility for the tribal tracts should be entrusted to the centre. In the subsequent years and upto 1947 numerous Acts and Regulations were promulgated and various reforms introduced. Thus in 1935 more stringent regulations providing for a special treatment of the tribal areas were incorporated by converting them into "Totally and partially excluded Areas".

After 1947

With the dawn of independence, the nation witnessed a considerable awakening about the welfare of the tribal people. This was reflected in various provisions of the constitution. It visualised a policy of the progressive assimilation of the tribal people in the national mainstream. In order to promote the integration of the tribal people with the rest of their Indian brethren, the constitution provided special safeguards for the tribal communities for a period of ten years. This period continues getting further extension to this day. A tribal welfare department was instituted in 1951 for the protection and advancement of the scheduled tribes and with the help of various provisions of the constitution, a new line of administration was chalked out. Article 244 of the constitution provides for the administration of "Scheduled Areas" in accordance with the Fifth Schedule and (in Assam) "Tribal Areas" under sixth schedule.

The scheduled Area thus defined is administered as part of the states in which they are situated by the Governor, is given powers : (a) to modify central and state laws in their application to them (b) to frame regulations for their peace and good government in particular for the protection of the rights of tribal in land, the allotment of waste land and their protection from money lenders. In the framing of the regulations the Governor is required to constitute the Tribes Advisory Council in the State. The Governor is further required to submit to the President of India an annual report or a report at such interval as may be required by the Union Government. Thus in the constitution ample provisions exist to protect the rights of the tribal in land, from agrarian and money lenders exploitation. The scheduled areas have been constituted with two clear objectives. One is to assist the tribals in enjoying their existing rights and the second is to develop the scheduled areas and promote the economic, educational progress of scheduled tribes.

Administration under fifth schedule

The fifth schedule visualises a division of responsibility between the State Government and Union Government in the matter of administration of the scheduled Areas. The state Government is directed to screen legislation unsuitable for extension to the tribal areas and to frame regulations for peace and good government. It is also the responsibility of the State Government to implement special schemes of tribal welfare and general development of the scheduled tribes inhabiting its boundaries. The union Government takes the responsibility of providing guidance to the State Government regarding administration of the scheduled areas and also to make available additional funds required to raise the administrative capability and standard of living of the tribals. The Union Government also enjoys power to give direction to the State Government regarding the implementation of particular schemes, laying down priorities in their implementation and in regard to the general administration of the tribal areas.

The union government's responsibility for the administration of the scheduled Areas is not limited only to the provisions of funds for their development but extends to guiding the State Governments and giving directions to them. Their crucial role is provided for in Article 339 (2) and para 3 of the fifth schedule of the constitution relied on persuasion and the good sense of the State Government to adopt a uniform policy for development of Areas and rarely the situation demands a direction to the State Government. It is better if the poor tribals are not dragged in unnecessary bickerings and the tug of war between crucial administration agencies. Further periodical conferenes are held with the planning commission and the ministry of Home Affairs to review the progress in regard to the programmes and to consider difficulties in their implementation.

Laws in the Scheduled Areas

In the matter of laws applicable to scheduled Areas the Governor has been given power to make regulations for their peace and good government. He has also the power to direct that state and central laws shall not apply to the scheduled Areas or shall only apply with modifications.

Role of the Traditional Tribal Council and the Advent of Panchayat Raj

The functions of the institution of the traditional tribal society have been primarily to decide social and religious matters in the light of their customary laws and in some areas to determine judicial matters also on the basis of the consent of the people as a whole. This does not mean that the tribal council did not decide economic questions. This has been a part of their social responsibility. These tribal councils were not elected bodies. Hereditary was often the basis but many a time character of the personal life of an individual elevated him to his counter position. Despite such constraints every adult had an equal right to argue and put forth any question and thus issues used to be settled through consensus. The decision of the councils are law to the tribals because they are based on their social customs and religious rites.

In one of my studies (Dimensions of Development in Tribal Bihar, Inter India, 1986) it has been found that Introduction of statutory Panchayati System through out India has weakened the traditional tribal panchayat but in most of the cases statutory panchayat are discharging all those functions which were done by the traditional panchayat. In addition statutory panchayats are also executing developmental schemes. It has been further found that the statutory and the traditional panchayat are functioning side by side/together and the office bearers are also the same.

The Constitutional Safeguards under the Tribal Plans

About three decades ago the panchayat policy of tribal transformation was enunciated by the first Prime Minister Sri Jawaharlal Nehru ; the first of the five principles being that development should be along the lines of the genius of the tribal community and nothing should be imposed on them. The Scheduled Areas and Scheduled tribes commission set up under the chairmanship of Shri U.N. Dhebar in 1960 referred to this policy approvingly and observed that "The problem of problems is not to disturb the harmony of tribal life and simultaneously work for its advance ; not to impose anything upon the tribals and simultaneously work for their integration as members and part of the Indian family". A study team appointed by the Planning Commission headed by P. Shilu Ao (one time Chief Minister of Nagaland) opined that "the aim of tribal welfare policy should be defined as the progressive advancement, social and economic, of the tribals with a view to effecting their integration with the rest of the community on a footing of equality within a reasonable distance of time. The period has necessarily to vary from tribe to tribe and while it may be five or ten years in the case of certain tribes, more particularly the tribes that have already come into contact with the general population by living in the plans it may be two decades or more in the case of tribals who are still in the primitive "food-gathering stage".

The Dhebar Commission (1961) divided the scheduled tribes into four categories : those living in the remotest corners and for that reason almost in the primitive stage, those in the shifting cultivation stage, those who have taken to regular agriculture and, finally, those who have already been assimilated. They added that the differences in physical environment also call for separate treatment. The Shilu Ao Team (1969) thought that there were three principal groups of tribes in the country, at one end of the scale the tribes living in the vastnesses of the hills, cut off from contact, still in the hunting and food gathering stage, at the other end, the politically conscious and economically advanced communities of the north-east, and in between, the tribal communities of the country's central girdle in varying stage of development. Whatever classification is adopted, the fact remains that there is a wide divergenee in the socio-economic, cultural and technological milieu among the five hundred and fiftynine scheduled tribe communities of the country, calling for opposite treatment for each. Of late we have witnessed loud vioce of protest and dissent from certain segments of the national polity, nursing grievances of neglect of group identity and economic backwardness. There have been divisive tendencies. Prompt and adequate measures should be taken in the direction of preservation of the identity of the concerned groups as well as for their socio-economic advancement to avoid situations similar to that in the north-east.

It cannot be stressed too strongly that taking into consideration the psyche, personality, cultural milieu and level of socio-economic development of each tribe, distinctive plans for development will have to be formulated for the scheduled tribe communities. The project reports of ITDPs should reflect close relationship between the programmes and schemes suggested and the individuality of the communities covered. Undoubtedly, this would require a comparatively high degree of perception and expertise for which not only the right attitude but also appropriate training and orientation are indispensable. Similarly, the state tribal sub-plan should mirror the needs and aspirations of the concerned sections of the population as well as the local natural resource endowment projects and plans based on different premises would not hold relevance.

Constitutional Provisions

Article 46 of the consitution enjoins on the states to promote with special care the educational and economic interests of the weaker sections of the people, and, in particular, of the scheduled castes and the scheduled tribes, and to protect them from social injustice and all forms of exploitation. Some other provisions enable the President to make arrangement for implementation of the objective set forth in Article 46. Article 244 empowers him to declare an area as a scheduled or Tribal Area under the Fifth Schedule and (or) the Sixth Schedule separately. Under the Fifth Schedule, the Governor has been vested with the authority to modify state and central laws and to make Regulations for peace and good government of Scheduled Areas.

Article 339 (2) lays down that the executive power of the union extends to the giving of directions to a state as to the drawing up and execution of schemes for the welfare of the scheduled tribes in the state. Further, paragraph 3 of part A of the Fifth schedule provides that the executive power of the Union shall extend to the giving of directions to the states as to the administration of scheduled Areas. Article 275 provides for financial assistance to state for implementation of schemes of development of scheduled tribes and raising the level of administration in the scheduled Areas. Articles 15, 16 and and 19 make it possible, while legislating on any matter to take into consideration the special conditions of tribals in the matter of enforcing the provisions relating to equality of all citizens.

It would thus appear that while the scheduled Areas are to be administered as part of the state in which they are situated, wide powers have been conferred on the Governor for their administration. He has been enabled to modify central state laws in their application to them and to frame Regulations for the peace and good government and, in particular, for the protection of the rights of tribals in land, the allotment of waste land and their protection from money-lenders. He is required to consult the Tribes Advisory Council in the state in framing of these Regulations. Notwithstanding such powers land alienation continues to take place, usury is rampant and incidence of bonded labour does not appear to have substantialy abated.

The Objective and Strategy

Even as early as 1959, the Renuka Ray report emphasised that while each aspect of development was important in its own place integrated programmes based on agriculture, forestry, handicrafts and village industries were needed, the degree of emphasis upon each of them being determined by a systematic survey of the needs and possibilities in each area. The Dhebar Commission stressed integrated approach. According to them the problem of economic development for the bulk of the tribals cannot be solved unless the resources of land, forests, cattle wealth, cottage and village industries are all executed on an integrated basis. However, apart from touching on the broad strategy and indicating socio-economic development as a general goal, no specific objective was spelt out. The Fourth Five Year Plan (1969-74) document enumerated that the "problem of Scheduled tribes living in compact areas is essentially that of economic development of their areas and of integrating their economy with that of the country". The expert committee set up in 1972 under the chairmanship of S.C. Dubey for advising on formulation of new strategy during the Fifth Five Year Plan defined the task of tribal development as social and economic development of the tribals through fast and time bound integrated area development and other programmes suiting the genius of the people, progressive elimination of all forms of exploitation and ensuring a move towards the goals of equality and justice. The last cited formulation went further than many of its predecessors, yet it seems to have been generally framed. The objective spelt out by the Planning Commission were less specialised (1) narrowing the gap between the level of development of tribals and other areas and (ii) improving the quality of the tribal communities. "Quality of life" lent itself to diverse interpretations.

Some of the drawbaeks in policies and programmes of tribal development, following up to the end of the last plan noticed were: (a) since many sectoral programmes for executing schemes were dependant on the limited resources of the backward classes welfare sector they got atrophied financially and physically (b) there was failure to comprehend distinctive characteristics of the tribal areas and the scheduled tribes and (c) the policies and programmes as well as the administrative machinery therefore hardly moulded to their needs. The Government of India took the decision that from the Fifth Plan onwards the major thrust for development of the tribal areas and tribal communities ought to be provided by each of the concerned sectoral authorities. Since sometimes area development was provided for at the cost of the tribal community, it was laid down that the strategy would be area development with focus on development of the tribal communities.... for areas where tribals are a predominant community". The tasks were defined as elimination of exploitation in all forms, spreading up the process of socio-economic development building inner strength of the people and improving their organizational capacity.

The problem was broadly divided into (1) areas of tribal socio-economic development, building inner strength of the former, the concept of area development with focus on development of the tribal communities has been maintained. In respect of the latter, on particular scheme of infrastructural development for aiding tribal development specially is feasible since the infrastructural would support development schemes of all section of people, tribal development in such a situation should comprise community based schemes sustained in the matrix of general infrastructural development schemes.

The strategy for integrated development led to the launching of the tribal sub-plan concept in the Fifth plan period. Three basic parameters in the tribal situation in the country were recognised in the formulation of the concept. First, that there is variation in the social, political, economic and cultural milieu among the different scheduled tribe communities in the country. Second, that their demographic distribution reveals their concentration in parts of the same states and dispersal in others. Third, that the primitive tribal communities live in scheduled regions. Hence, the broad approach to tribal development has had to be related to their level of development of tribal communities orinted programmes have been preferred. The dispersed tribals found in pocket have to avail of the programmes of rural development but the *Block* agency can introduce in such programmes an apt bias to meet their specific needs. For execution of programmes having integrated thrust pooling of financcs from all sector has been regarded as an essential requisite.

Experience of planning has shown that nearly 50% to 70% of the State's plan budget is tied up for capital intensive sectoral programmes like power, flood control, large and medium industries, mining and transportation, living a balance pool to be shared among the non-tribal and the tribal systems of the state's population and administrative costs. In effect it means that family oriented schemes liable to make substantial difference to the income of the tribal family are at a discount. It has been calculated that the range of percentage of funds earmarked for beneficiary oriented programmes is between 0.02 to 15.66 mostly in the neighbourhood 0% to 5%. The planning process tends to be reoriented to acquire a basis in favour of beneficiary oriented schemes.

We feel that the time has now come to set before the administration some concretised objectives so that their realisation can also be distinctly tangible. While reaffirming that the identity had cultural milieu of individual tribal communities need to be preserved and fostered. We feel that the most urgent tasks should be to create in the economic field impact of an order which will enable to targeted number of families belonging to a scheduled tribe community to cross the poverty line. In other words, this would mean increase in productivity levels in the fields of agriculture, horticulture, animal husbandry, forestry, industry etc. Provision of employment in the slack season and above all, ending exploitation in the credit cum marketing field. The strategies in the respective fields have to be worked out by each state Government in detail. The poverty line at 1979-80 prices have been placed by the plan ning commission at the figure of Rs. 75 per capita per month. The magnitude of the efforts to be mounted by the concerned ITDPS in a state will have to be qualitatively and quantitatively related to the gap between the present income level and the poverty line. Benchmark surveys have already been conducted for tribal subplan areas in some of the states and these should yield reasonably reliable data regarding the present per capita income. In states where the benchmark surveys have not been conducted or have been lagging behind, quick sample surveys should lead to a reasonable close figure of per capita income. The formulation must spell out programmes and schemes along with the likely accrual to the families of benefits in financial terms, exhibiting phrase for gradual bridging of the gap.

The tribal sub-plan aims at comprehensive development with focus on the individual family. In line with the assault on poverty, those families living below the poverty line whether belonging to the scheduled tribe communities or not, would need to be identified, their needs and problems assessed and programmes executed. With the households as the basic unit of planning in poverty reduction the poorest and therefore poor on a programme scale should be taken up. With the predominance in tribal areas of agriculture land being regarded as the basic resource asset, landless agricultural labour should constitute the first target group for benefiting the marginal and the small farmers. In rural tribal areas income from forest product should be kept in view in identifying the poorest, the poor and so on. In the urban areas, the unorganised unskilled group of mining industrial etc. labour should be the focus of attention.

Apart from core economic sectors like agriculture, animal husbandry, horticulture etc. education will not merely equip the tribals for job opportunities, but it is an essential acquisition for survival of many of the scheduled tribe communities. They have had little interface with the modern system prevalent outside the tribal areas which places them in a position of serious disadvantage. Both through the formal and non-formal education the window that may be opened should enable them to come to grips with the outside world with some degree of confidence, whereafter only they may be able to convert education into an economic asset. We regard education, therefore, as a key sector for the seventh plan.

The idea of totality in tribal sub-plan is fundamental. In other words, the totality of effort in integrated tribal development project has to be undertaken with the totality of resources. In the past, the tribal areas have been deprived of their due share of funds. The infrastructure was poorly laid and hence absorption capacity was also low, investment was inhibited. Lack of investment kept the infrastructure stagnant. The vicious circle can be broken only by determined, quantified investments in the tribal areas for infrastructure and individual family development from the central and state plans as well as institutional finance. An effort in this regard was initiated in the sixth plan and that needs to be carried out systematically and thoroughly. We understand that the central ministries, having begun the exercise, have yet to bring it to its logical conclusion. We trust that this will be done expeditiously.

Earlier the exploitation of the tribals has been referred to. However the problem of exploitation in tribal areas is widespread and acute. As yet, no reliable estimate of loss of the basic resources of the tribal, i.e. the land, has been made but considering that his land has been taken away by the Government, public and private undertakings, individual enterprises and individuals for various purposes like townships, major and medium industries, and medium irrigation projects, mining complexes, roads etc. we have no doubt that the total quantum which might have gone out of his possession would be consider able. Serious efforts need to be made, therefore, for restoration of the land. Trade, commerce, middlemen etc. have exhibited a strong tendency to exploit the tribals. Liquor vendors have drained the tribal areas of their resources. Forest contractors have been employing tribal labour on less than the statutory minimum wage rate. In many instances, tribals have been reduc ed to bondage. Elimination of exploitation, particularly restoration of the basic lands resources to the tribal should be made as one of the major objective of the tribal development during the current plan period along with upgradation of the economic educational levels.

Therefore to sum up, the objectives of the current period is as follows :—

(a) Raising the productivity levels in the fields of agriculture, horticulture, animal husbandry, forestry, cottage, village and small industry, etc. so as to create an economic impact of an order which will enable to targeted number of families (say 50%) in the tribal sub-plan areas to across the poverty line. With the household as the basic Unit of planning in poverty reducation, the poorest and then the poor should be taken up on a progressive scale.

(b) Apart from the effort in the core economic sectors indicated in (a) above, education should become the key sector in the current plan period.

(c) The attainment of the objectives (a) and (b) above would vitally depend on an adequate infrastructure for the creation of which there should be commensurate financial and physical effort.

(d) Concomitant with the aforesaid threefold aim and perhaps the most important assiduous exertion of tribals in the fields of alienation of land, money lending, debt bondage, trade, excise, forest etc.

Coverage

During the last plan period, in certain major states of tribal concentration, a Block or Tehsil or a Taluka was chosen as the smallest unit for identifying the tribal majority units. This norm was applied to Gujarat, Himachal Pradesh, Madhya Pradesh, Orissa and Rajasthan. In some states it was difficult to come across development blocks or alternative units with more than 50% of tribal concentration as the tribal population was dispersed e.g. in Tamil Nadu, Kerala and Assam : a total population threshold of about 20,000 or other 10,000 was worked upon. But in some other states like West Bengal and Tripura, even this did not help and a group of villages each with more than 50% of tribal population had to be considered for inclusion. Some adjustments were made later, with the result that by the end of the last plan period, about 65% of the total scheduled tribe population of the country was covered by the tribal sub-plans. The attempt in the last plan period was to extend the coverage further, by going down to a unit lower than a block. Pockets of a minimum of 10,000 total population with 5o% or more of scheduled tribe population, have been identified in various states and with their exercise 75% of the total scheduled tribe population in the country is expected to be covered. The exercise in identification of pockets of tribal concentration has been completed for the states of Andhra Pradesh, Bihar, Gujarat, Maharashtra, Madhya Pradesh, Rajasthan and Uttar Pradesh. In respect of Orissa the process is yet to be completed.

Methodology of Preparation of Tribal Sub-plan

Since the strategy is to prepare programmes for the specific needs of the area and the people, planning has to start from the lowest unit i.e. ITDP. Each constituent block of an ITDP should formulate its five year plan with annual phasing in the context of the natural resources endowment, occupations and skills of the people, infrastructure and human requirement etc. Since the block plans will be circumscribed in their jurisdiction, their utility in infrastructural planning may be limited but they will form valuable planning base in respect of beneficiary oriented schemes. The block plans should be coordinated and aggregated at the ITDP level, taking an overview of the entire project area. The project report thus prepared should be integrated and aggregated at the state level into the Tribal sub-plan of the State. The need based ITDP project report and the state sub-plan have to be matched to resource availability. The process of planning has, thus to built up upwards. The process needs to be initiated simultaneously at the ITDP and the State level. Interviewing of the sectoral programmes has to take place at the block, the ITDP as well as the state levels. In other words, the project report for and ITDP should reflect balanced inter sectoral programmes relative to the natural resource endowment, the skills and aptitudes of the people. The tribal sub-plan for a state should represent an aggregate of the various project reports, articulating in sum the priorities, needs and aspirations of the tribal areas in state, duly married to the financial resources available.

The methodology, implies that the state authorities communicate to the project anthorities outlays for the five year period as well as for each of the one year phases before the commencement of the respective periods. Once the outlays are known, the project authorities have to sort out priorities and this stage, particularly association of tribal representatives is of crucial importance so that the plans can become truly reflective of the people's needs, aspirations and inclinations. Presently, generally, the disaggregation exercise is adopted whereby the lump sectoral outlays are broken up and passed on to the concerned field authorities for implementation of programmes. Since the process plans from below has not come into being completely in any of the states, efforts have to be made to streamline it and for it to become a full reality. In essence planning from below implying realistic integrated effort has to be kept in the fore.

Development Strategy for Tribal Pockets

Pockets outside the current sub-plan area having tribal concentration are proposed to be added to the tribal sub-plan area. The two criteria are that each of such pocket should have a minimum of 10,000 of total population out of which not less than 50% should be scheduled tribe population. Such pocket should form a part of Development block or in states like Maharashtra and Gujarat a Taluk. As indicated, except in case of Orissa, other concerned states have finalised the pockets lying outside the present sub-plan area. The thrust of development of infrastructure and of many other programmes should come from the financial and physical. However, the small community in pocket will specifically require to be looked after and for their purpose funds should be supplemented by the special central assistance of the Ministry of Home Affairs. The programmes drawn up should have community or a family orientation. For example, if basket weaving members constitute a scheduled tribe community e.g. the Kolgha in Gujarat, the programmes should be tailored to bring the maximum benefits in that occupation. A shifting cultivator trible like Sauria Paharia of Bihar will have to be treated suitably. On the other hand, if there is no general occupational pattern or otherwise no distinctive feature is discernible, schemes of socio-economic benefits of individual families should be taken in hand. In other word, in pockets of tribal concentration the thrust should be towards raising the socio-economic standard of individual tribal family.

Primitive Tribal Groups

The primitive groups are those who are at the extreme end of the scale, engaged for living in pre-agricultural pursuits like food gathering, fruit gathering, hunting, fishing etc. along with some amount of agriculture. They inhabit remote inaccessible area, cut off from the mainstream. The examples are the Sauria Paharia of Bihar, Yanadi of Andhra Pradesh, Saora of Orissa, Jarawa, and Onge of Andaman and Nicobar Islands.

The primitive groups require sensible and delicate handling, separate project reports for each of such communities. The project report should devote adequate attention to their special problems. Separate administrative structure for their development is necessary.

Anti-exploitative Measures

The scheduled tribe communities will be able to grasp the fruits of socio-economic measures in proposition to the dispatch employed by the delivery system. Actual experience, generally, is of slow dispatch. But the anti-exploitative steps can transmit the benefits much more quickly with less effort, such steps comprises very simple measures like (a) giving the tribals the due price for their farm and forest produce relieving them from the clutches of the traders, merchants and middlemen (b) providing them their consumer necessities at reasonable or controlled prices, rescuing them from the vice of the village Bania or Mufassil middlemen (c) allowing them production and consumption credit at reasonable rate of interest instead of the usurious rates charged by the moneylenders. Large sized multipurpose cooperative societies (LAMPS) have been thought to be a fit instrument.

Alienation of land belonging to tribals continues to be a serious problem. Particularly in the central mining cum industrial belt from Durgapur, Bokaro, Ranchi, Jamshedpur, Rourkela, Bhilai etc. With the practice of subsistence economy, the perpetual want is expensively satisfied by usurious money lenders, often resulting in loss of the basic resource, i.e. land. These conditions have led in many cases to labour bondage. Many states have framed regulation under the fifth schedule of the constitution or enacted laws otherwise for curbing these evils. In the industrialising and mining areas, exploitation of tribal labour is rampant and the state Government is yet to come up with some firm rules and regulations. This need due consideration and 'real' will of the administrative machinery.

Planned Development and Approaches to Tribal Problems

The tribe is a system of social organisation which includes several local groups—villages, bands, districts, lineages and normally includes a common territory, a common language and a common culture. The elements constituting the tribe may or may not be coordinated by formal or centralized political power. Ideally the term implies a large element of solidarity based on strongly shared primary sentiments. Such solidarity becomes contractual in nature as the tribal organization becomes more formally organised. The point at which these latter characteristics become pronounced is, perhaps a convenient place to distinguish between the tribe and the nation. In general, anthropologists agree on the criteria by which a tribe may be described are (i) common territory (ii) a tradition of common descent (iii) common language (iv) common culture (v) a common name (vi) own political system and (vii) simple economy. A scheduled tribe is he who is scheduled in article 342 of the Indian Constitution.

Social scientists, planners and administrators are more concerned with the development of peasants and tribals who all live in the so-called "primitive society". Indian anthropology deals with the study of inhabitants of primitive society. Indian anthropologists have been concerned with microlevel studies of tribal and rural communities, and their knowledge of the processes and problems of socio-cultural change appears to be promising. They seem to be best equipped to help planners and administrators to deal with development of the aforesaid categories of people. But how far they are being considered relevant in planning development programmes needs to be considered seriously by the self-styled academicians. Let anthropology and anthropologist be now not allowed to be used only as a show piece of the drawing room.

Tribal development consists of deliberate efforts by the tribals along with the planners, anthropologists and the elite groups to orient them towards the new cultural and social ways of life and action by the tribals is no longer tribal development. When the tribals feel that the quality of life to which they aspire is in fact achieved, we may claim it to be tribal development.

It may sound impossible to some of us to attain the level. In reality it depends on how we approach the basic problems of the tribals. Over the years, since the advent of planning age we have been working out strategies to improve the socio-economic conditions of weaker sections and for development of the vulnerable groups. The poor, weaker, peasantry and slum dwellers were the pet subject of discussion for planners, professors and politicians until very recently. Out of gross vacillation or inability to deal effectively with their problems, the emphasis seems to have shifted very recently towards the dearest of our weaker sections, namely the 'scheduled tribes'.

Another important role of anthropologists is to research and advise on the impact of technology and innovations, the personal or social consequences of planned change and "development" or of "progress" such impact studies seek to protect and enhance the welfare and quality of life of those most vulnerable to the impact of technology and innovations those among whom these are introduced and promoted. Their information can also be to soften or divert, redirect or prevent the undesirable consequences of innovations, in the hope of enabling the survival of people in society worth inhabiting.

Study of change, may be rural or tribal or urban, continues to be a favourite field of study for anthropologists. Anthropological studies differ from other studies by economists, political scientists and journalists in the sense that the anthropologists use more scientific methods such as participant observation which is considered to be an essential element of social anthropology aiming to get intimate and first hand information about rural communities. No amount of book knowledge is considered to be equal to the intensive fieldwork, experience of an anthropologist. The scientist usually deals with large areas or with great number of people and their experiences differ from that of an anthropologist. They do not generally possess the first hand information and ambiguity between investigators (often untrained) and report writing experts results in supply of wrong information and ineffective depiction of empirical reality leading to wrong conclusions in many cases. Various anthropologists interpret participant observation as a technique to participate in community activities in order to observe and understand the social reality around him. According to Beatille and Madan (1975 : 5-6) "Fieldwork is an amalgam of methodological rigour and the unpredictable consequences of the personality of observer". There is no clearcut formula for handling any given field situation, for each situation is unique. The field worker is expected to arrive at his own equation with his objects.

The nature of theory in anthropological studies has not been viewed rigorously by the research methodologies and remains in a confused state. Various anthropologists view it differently.

India is one of the few nations noted for tribal concentration. According to 1981 census, the tribals of India account for 7.18 per cent of the total population. About 80 per cent of them live in remote forest areas and hill tracts without any access to modern socio-economic inputs.

Although articles 15 (4), 224(i) and 339 of the constitution speak of special provisions meant for the administration and control of scheduled Areas and Tribals therein, for their welfare and protection, except for commissions and reports, the executive power at the action level has done practically nothing to improve their socio-economic condition of course, many explanations have been advanced for their failures, but these do not seem to point to the culpability of tribal welfare departments and their protectors, just as the Harijans literal meaning children of God referred to in the special provisions of our constitution have become a means of exploitation for all who are connected with their welfare or "illfare".

Even after forty years of Independence, the tribals continue to remain untouched by the general prosperity of the nation and still in the lowest strata of society. Their way of living is a challenge to modern civilization. They have been subjected to various types of exploitation for generations and their life is characterised by servitude, poverty and misery. Generally speaking, they are still under the clutches of their centuries old traditions and inimical customs. They are in the firm grip of a subsistence economy and indebtedness is the hallmark of tribal existence in India.

'Action Oriented' researches were conducted under the expert guidance of an eminent scholar wedded to tribal life and dedicated to the welfare of the weaker sections. Consequently, the volume of 'Reports' increased at an alarming pace along with the number of Institutes and Directors, Joint Directors, Deputy Directors, Additional Directors, Assistant Directors and Special Executive Directors. But at the end of it all, the only comment that can be made is : "Poor are my tribals, rich are their projectors". This is the net result of the welfare programmes. And it is a fact that the more the plans, the more the tribals are moving from 'poverty to absolute pamperism'. What they need is not expert seminars, comprehensive reports or directives from Ministers and Ministries, but a time bound solution to their centuries old socio-economic problems. Nevertheless, credit does go to the planners for what they have been able to do.

The findings of my empirical study undertaken during 1980, 1981-83 and 1984-85 on a primitive tribe of Bihar i.e. Sauria Paharia is that economically they are yet quite backward in spite of the special, component and general VIth plan of the country and something tangible is yet to be brought for them with the help of VIIth national and some component plans. Though according to census reports Sauria Paharia population has been virtually stagnant at around 57,000 since 1911. A recent study of mine indicates that it is actually declining. A look at the total population of Sauria Paharia also suggests that they are the only scheduled tribe whose pouulation has consistently been falling from 1931, though the rate of decrease has been slow, —2.1 per cent in 1931-41 and —5.1 per cent in 1941-61.

A system of medicine may be viewed as an institutional apparatus of defence against the incursion of pain and ever-looming threat of annihilation that is the human lot. Most of the ethnographic reports prepared by various anthropologists of Indian tribe refer to the belief of the concerned tribe about their short and long illnesses and their traditional method of curing them from such disease but none of them have carried out a medical test on their respondents. A medical check up of the sample population have been carried out. They believe that if a spirit, may be of the village or of the family, becomes unhappy one suffers from Malaria, T.B., Cholera, Leprosy and such other diseases. They have their own method of treating these diseases. In most of the cases they go to the Ojha, worship, use home medicine and herbs for any kind of disease and treatment prevalent among Sauria Paharias. A Vaidya (Ayurvedic Doctor) has been appointed by a voluntary organisation for the treatment of the Paharia of Borio Block. But the said Vaidya sits only in the weekly market of the Borio whereas the Sauria Paharias reside on the hill tops. None of the respondents of the villages under study have gone even once to him for his treatment. The study further reveals that none of them have ever availed of allopathic medical facilities extended to them through various plans of the nation. May be because the hospitals are located in administrative headquarters whereas the beneficiaries reside at the hill tops and also because the qualified medical practitioners have never visited to them. The most interesting thing is that they have no idea of this Block. Barring a few Paharia elites none of them could come out with the name of their Blocks. Their poor economic condition also checks them from taking any treatment or medicine.

In their economic life, Sabai grass (*Jechamum angusti flinm*) plays an important role. The grass has long life, but the quality remains good for the first 15 or 16 years only. Subsequently it gradually falls. Earlier the market was secured for the Paharias by the mass purchase of all their grass by the Titagarh Paper Mills, Calcutta but now it is managed by the Forest department. The welfare department has been making a grant of Rs. 55 lakh to the Forest department for managing Sabai cultivation since 1962. In 1961, Forest department was able to organise such cultivation in 15,000 acres but with the rise in labour costs and enhancement of salaries, T.A. and D.A. of the Staff, the department has now restricted its operations to only 2,500 acres. Sabai grass is grown on the lands of the Paharias for which each family gets a royalty. The average royalty per family is Rs. 58.92 per annum which is quity meagre. The new schemes introduced by the Government assures 87 paise per maund to the Paharias even when there is a threat of loss. Even this is considered negligble. They are not hired to work as labour in Sabaibari. They feel no involvement in the work. It seems that they are dissatisfied with the control and management of Sabai production by the Forest department officials. The forests supplement the Khallu economy of Paharia in many ways like royalty of Sabai, edible roots and fruits, bamboo, firewood, forest fruits used for commercial purposes etc.

Being primitive and economically backward the Paharias are more vulnerable to exploitation. They are exploited by Mahajans, police officials, Block officials, Santhals and other tribals, by non-tribals (specially in the market) and also by their own elites. The Mahajans play a vital role in their economy. Sauria Paharia are in habit of taking loans from them. They generally take loans at on the accasions at clearing the jungle, sowing, harvesting, marriage, death and religious ceremonies. The Paharias say that once they take loan from the Mahajans it is difficult to free themselves from debt because the interest goes on multiplying every year. Fifty per cent interest is charged for cash loans while hundred per cent is charged for loans in kind. The little pieces of land that they still have are cultivated in the majority of cases by Santhal or Hindu mahajans mostly for the loan of Rs. five or ten.

They are often exploited by police officials. Mahesh Malto, Chulwa Paharia, Mesa Paharia and others of Karam Pahar said that when even there was a series of theft in Sahebganj town or in adjacent places, police officials arrested them without giving any reason. In fact they are never involved in such cases. Many Sauria Paharias are in Sahebganj or Dumka jails for no reason. Being poor they are unable to engage a lawyer. They also feel that they are being exploited by forest officials. Mahesh Malto feels that Sabaibari is not being used properly and its royalty is also not distributed properly. He was critical of the Paharia welfare officer who had never visited the cluster of five villages. They get very low price of their products in the market. In most of the cases such low prices are not paid even in full. It so happens that the prices are paid in small coins in which they have difficulty in calculating the price. Traders take advantage of their ignorance and the prices paid to them are invariably lesser than the fixed one by the traders. Some non-tribals have taken the land of the Paharia on lease for mining purposes. This destroys the Sabai cultivation area. In this case Paharias are also exploited because they get a paltry amount for the mining lease. Some non-tribals and Santhals frequently go to the Paharia villages either to steal their fruits or to cut the bamboo plantations or other trees of which they are rightful owners. Even if they are aware of their exploitation, they are unable to do anything in this regard in the absence of any credit agency.

There are a few clever one among the Sauria Paharia themselves who exploit their brethern by lending cash or food grains, for which they charge interest like regular money lenders. This kind of exploitation is beyond the purview of money lending act. No systematic study has been done on this aspect. Article 342 of the Indian Constitution provides similar facilities for each tribe but the 'Elites' or the 'neo-tribes' are posing more problems for their own brethren as well as for the planners and administrators. The anthropologists' role of

'Social Doctor' is required more here to heal their burns otherwise this may pose a problem in future. So far many researches have been done on the exploitation of tribals by the *non-tribals but the exploitation of the tribals by the tribals has not yet been done. This may be considered as one of the gift* of the planned development. Because in most of such plans the knowledge of the specialists has been ignored and their reports have been treated as an item of luxury by the planners and administrators.

Though the planned development aimed at strategic development of a tribe/caste/community region through various developmental inputs but the output of the last six planned developments demonstrate specially in the field of tribal development, that the target development is a far cry. A number of reasons may be assigned for it but the real crux of the problem is that the subject and the area specialists have never been accommodated while designing such developmental plans. For example, many agencies like UNICEF, Deepayaten, welfare and various other departments of the government have provided various developmental inputs, amounting in total to several crores, but all those inputs proved to be useless and hoax. Not because they do not have expertise but simply because they never coordinated with SUBJECT and AREA Specialists. Anthropologist of today has to play a very important role in the development of the country, especially of the tribals, otherwise the future generation will always raise their finger and will question their role. Anthropologists should begin their heart searching for the kind of researches in which they are involved today.